7/02

DATE DUE

BRODART, CO.   Cat. No. 23-221-003

The Korean War

⊣ ALSO BY THE AUTHORS ⊢

By Donald M. Goldstein and Katherine V. Dillon:

The Williwaw War (1992)

The Pearl Harbor Papers: Inside the Japanese Plans (1993)

Amelia: The Centennial Biography of an Aviation Pioneer (1997)

By Donald M. Goldstein and Katherine V. Dillon, with
   J. Michael Wenger:

The Way It Was: Pearl Harbor: The Original Photographs (1991)

D-Day Normandy: The Story and Photographs (1993)

"Nuts!" The Battle of the Bulge: The Story and Photographs (1994)

Rain of Ruin: The Hiroshima and Nagasaki Atomic Bombs (1995)

The Vietnam War: The Story and Photographs (1997)

The Spanish-American War: The Story and Photographs (1998)

By Donald M. Goldstein and Katherine V. Dillon, with
   Gordon W. Prange:

At Dawn We Slept: The Untold Story of Pearl Harbor (1981)

Miracle at Midway (1982)

Target Tokyo: The Story of the Sorge Spy Ring (1984)

Pearl Harbor: The Verdict of History (1987)

December 7, 1941: The Day the Japanese Attacked Pearl Harbor (1988)

God's Samurai: Lead Pilot at Pearl Harbor (1990)

By Donald M. Goldstein and Katherine V. Dillon, with
   Masataka Chihaya:

Fading Victory: The Diary of Admiral Matome Ugaki (1991)

By Donald M. Goldstein, Phil Williams, and J. M. Shafritz:

Classic Readings of International Relations (1998)

By Donald M. Goldstein, Phil Williams, and Hank Andrews:

Security in Korea: War, Stalemate and Negation (1994)

By Harry J. Maihafer:

From the Hudson to the Yalu: West Point '49 in the Korean War (1993)

*Brave Decisions: Moral Courage from the Revolutionary War to
   Desert Storm* (1995)

Oblivion: The Mystery of West Point Cadet Richard Cox (1997)

*The General and the Journalists: Ulysses S. Grant, Horace Greeley,
   and Charles Dana* (1998)

The Korean War
The Story and Photographs

DONALD M. GOLDSTEIN
HARRY J. MAIHAFER

BRASSEY'S
WASHINGTON, D.C.

Map on p. 3 from *In Mortal Combat,* by John Toland; copyright ©1991 by John Toland; reprinted by permission of HarperCollins Publishers, Inc. Map on p. 6 by Jay Karamales.

Library of Congress Cataloging-in-Publication Data
Goldstein, Donald M.
    The Korean War: the story and photographs/Donald M. Goldstein, Harry J.
Maihafer.—1st ed.
        p. cm.
    Includes bibliographical references and index.
    ISBN 1-57488-217-1 (alk. paper)
    1. Korean War, 1950–1953—Pictorial works. 2. Korean War, 1950–1953. I. Maihafer,
Harry J. (Harry James), 1924– II. Title.

DS918.15 .G65 2000
951.904′2—dc21
                                                                                                    99-086416

Printed in the United States of America on acid-free paper that meets the American National Standards Institute Z39-48 Standard.

Brassey's
22841 Quicksilver Drive
Dulles, Virginia 20166

First Edition

10 9 8 7 6 5 4 3 2

CONTENTS

⊣MAPS⊢

⊣ PREFACE ⊢

This is the seventh in Brassey's series of photographic books titled "America Goes to War." The previous volumes were *The Way It Was: Pearl Harbor, D-Day Normandy, "Nuts!": The Battle of the Bulge, Rain of Ruin: A Photographic History of Hiroshima and Nagasaki, The Vietnam War*, and *The Spanish-American War*. This book is unique in that it is the first in the series coauthored by Harry J. Maihafer, a West Point graduate, a retired Army colonel, and a combat veteran of the Korean War.

We divided the current volume into ten chapters. Chapter 1, "The Land of the Morning Calm," describes the topography, geography, and early history of Korea. Chapter 2, "Prelude to War," presents the order of battle of the armed forces of North Korea and South Korea and the cast of characters preceding the war. Chapter 3, "South to the Naktong," relates the first phase of the war, the North Koreans' early victories, and the role of Task Force Smith in attempting to stem the tide. Chapter 4, "The Pusan Perimeter," depicts the United Nations (UN) forces' darkest hour as they struggle to "stand or die." Chapter 5, "Inchon," shows Gen. Douglas MacArthur's finest hour. After relating the planning and execution of the Inchon amphibious landing, the chapter concludes with the breakout from the Pusan Perimeter and the Allied decision to cross the 38th Parallel. Chapter 6, "North to the Yalu," describes the high water mark of the U.S. Eighth Army and the decision of the Peoples Republic of China to enter the war. Chapter 7, "The New War," relates the retreat of the UN forces from North Korea, the role of Matthew Ridgway as he reinvigorates and inspires a weary Eighth Army, the firing of MacArthur, and the closing days of the war of maneuver. Chapter 8, "The Tools of War," depicts some of the equipment used by the forces of both adversaries. Chapter 9, "The Static War," describes the harsh fighting that took place during the latter half of the war, the negotiations at Kaesong and Panmunjom, the prisoner exchanges, and the events leading to the final truce. Chapter 10, "Aftermath," praises the UN Allies; describes the economic miracle that is present-day South Korea; and portrays the Korean War Monument in Washington, D.C., that was dedicated in 1995.

Although we attempt to present the story of the Korean War in the context of its political and diplomatic background and with some analysis of what the Allies and the Republic of Korea (ROK) accomplished, our focus is primarily on the American fighting man, the one who bore the burden of the war, and who all too often, in the face of indifference at home, failed to receive the recognition he so richly deserved.

All photographs in this book are in the public domain. They are located at the National Archives, College Park, Maryland; the Naval Historical Center, Washington, D.C.; the Army War College, Carlisle Barracks, Pennsylvania; the Soldiers and Sailors Hall, Pittsburgh, Pennsylvania; or the Matthew B. Ridgway Center, University of Pittsburgh, or they are the personal property of the authors. Queries about the latter should be directed to Donald M. Goldstein.

We gratefully acknowledge the help and encouragement of Joe Dugan, Director, Soldiers and Sailors Hall; Robert Cressman, Naval Historical Center; Phil Williams, Ph.D., Director, Matthew B. Ridgway Center; Roy E. Wikman; Bunghee Kim; Dae Huan Kim; and James Enos. We are also grateful to Chris Dishman, Andrew Brinser, and Wendy Simkulak for their help in researching the book and to Tom Copeland and Doug Brooks of the Matthew B. Ridgway Center for their support and encouragement. Special thanks go to Katherine V. Dillon, Donald Goldstein's longtime partner and coauthor, who read the manuscript and made her comments; to Kendall Stanley for her typing and editing; and to Don McKeon, our man at Brassey's, who made it all happen.

We respectfully dedicate this book to the Americans and their Allied comrades who served in the Korean War and, especially, to those who failed to return.

Donald M. Goldstein, Ph.D. Col. Harry J. Maihafer, USA (Ret.)
Professor of Public and Nashville, Tennessee
   International Affairs
University of Pittsburgh
Pittsburgh, Pennsylvania

⊣ INTRODUCTION ⊢

Fifty years have passed since the Korean War began, and there has been no dearth of books about it. Monuments have been springing up all over America, and, in the nation's capital, the Korean War Memorial is one of the most frequently visited of all Washington sites. Yet, in the annals of American military history, the Korean War has the stigma of being called the "forgotten war," one that many say has slipped through the cracks of history. Fought between what some historians call "The Good War" (World War II) and "The Bad War" (Vietnam), the Korean War, until recently, has been neglected. Yet, with more than fifty-four thousand Americans killed and more than eight thousand missing in action in a war that lasted only three years, as opposed to one that lasted fifteen years, its casualties rank with those of the Vietnam War.

The Korean War was fought by many of the same military personnel who had also participated in World War II and by the same group that author and newscaster Tom Brokaw dubbed "the greatest generation." For the first time in American military history, the United States did not achieve absolute victory, that may be a reason for the war's "forgotten" title. To those who fought there, however, it was a terrible war, in a terrible place— a place where temperatures reached 30 degrees below zero, and where men were laid low not only by bullets but by frostbite and disease.

The Korean War was the first war fought by UN forces consisting of a coalition from nineteen countries. It was the first in which jet aircraft flew combat missions against each other and the first of many skirmishes in the Cold War between the communists and the United States. The war introduced brainwashing in the treatment of prisoners and brought about a reshaping of U.S. military policy.

Fifty years after the beginning of the war, this book is being published as the two Korean governments, North and South, are instituting a dialogue for change. The Korean Peninsula, however, remains partitioned, militarized, and volatile. With North Korea's reluctance to abide by the Nuclear Nonproliferation Treaty, its testing of missiles, and its unwillingness to permit inspection of its nuclear facilities, North Korea and rogue states, such as Iraq, create a situation with disastrous potential, even worse than that which existed during the limited war of the 1950s. The Korean Peninsula indeed remains high on the list of U.S. national security problems.

The past fifty years have seen reassessment of some of the more conventional interpretations of the war. The collapse of the Soviet Union and the opening of its archives in Moscow, the release of Chinese material about the war, and the availability of information in the United States under the Freedom of Information Act are all contributing to the process of reassessment. This new information has offered different insights to scholars, particularly regarding the onset of the war and Chinese intervention.

Even before the availability of this new information, however, the Korean War, like every war in U.S. history, has been subject to reassessment and controversial reinterpretation. Revisionist scholars, particularly those on the left, have argued very skillfully, often with an anti-American bias, that the conflict in Korea was domestic and that the Korean War was essentially a civil war transformed by the United States into a global conflict with Moscow. Scholars of all bents, moreover, have cited the vagaries of U.S. policy and have highlighted such mistakes as the failure in June 1950 to deter the North Korean attack and the subsequent failure to obtain early warning of the Chinese entry into the war. Volumes have been written on the Truman-MacArthur relationship, the political hysteria surrounding the alleged Democratic culpability for losing China, and the off-year congressional defeats caused by the war. These and other topics are discussed in the works listed in the Selected Bibliography of this book.

Thus, more than fifty years later, the heritage of the Korean War remains. The peninsula is still divided between diametrically opposed regimes. No peace treaty exists, only an armistice. Throughout the war, the communists were masters of propaganda; for example, they used the negotiations on prisoner exchange to maximum advantage. Similarly, they falsely accused the United States of germ warfare, and the Americans proved inept in countering the charge. The demilitarized zone, set up by the armistice, still exists. Today, there are more than thirty thousand U.S. military personnel in Korea who act as a trip wire. The war that was never legally declared has never legally ended.

In the classic sense, the United States did not win the Korean War. After the unconditional victory that ended World War II, the end of the Korean War seemed rather murky. President Harry S Truman had very strong support when the United States entered the war; however, with the Chinese entry into the conflict, he lost much of this support. Many American people turned against the war, but, unlike Vietnam, there was no burning of draft cards or flags, and no one, except a few extremists, was ready to fight China. In Korea, the United States demonstrated a loyalty and determination that greatly influenced its allies. Perhaps the war's greatest result was not how it might have contributed to the collapse of communism, which is certainly unclear, but that the United States drew a line in Korea. To the authors, this line seems to be the war's finest legacy. The justly famous war correspondent Ernie Pyle, who wrote about the soldiers of World War II, called them brave men. Those soldiers, however, were no braver than the soldiers who served in Korea and who had no Ernie Pyle to memorialize them. This is their story, told in photographs.

⊣ONE⊢
The "Land of the Morning Calm"

1–1 "Land of the Morning Calm."

1–3 Men of the 9th Infantry Regiment advancing up Hill 201.

They called Korea the "Land of the Morning Calm." Americans who served there also heard Korea's traditional name, Chosen. When winter hit, with typical GI humor, they dubbed it "Frozen Chosen." They had good reason.

This is a land of rich natural beauty, including scenery that sometimes approaches the spectacular (1–1). Men at war, however, were seldom in a position to appreciate that beauty. In any case, whatever the Americans thought of the landscape, no one, whether in summer or winter, had a good word for Korea's climate. The summers were hot, rainy, and humid. Temperatures could reach 110 degrees or higher, with humidity in the 90 percent range. Men, such as those in the work crew shown in photograph 1–2, suffered accordingly. Climbing Korea's steep hills and carrying a weapon and ammunition, often with a pack on one's back, was

1–2 American soldiers removing boulders to permit motorized vehicles to ford a stream.

1–4 Soldiers navigating rough terrain.

sheer torture (1–3, 1–4). New-comers often collapsed before reaching a summit, and, even if they made it to the top, there was always another hill lying just ahead. One wag suggested a Korean War motto: "Not this hill—the *next* one!" (1–5).

The winters, if possible, were even worse. Winds came whipping down out of Siberia, and, in the mountains where most of the fighting took place, there was a constant, numbing, icy chill (1–6). Staying in the open, especially at night, meant risking frostbite. On the other hand, if a man became too comfortable in his sleeping bag, he risked being surprised and killed by a merciless enemy.

Before 1950, few Americans could have located Korea on a map, much less described it. Where was this land of climatic extremes, and what was its topography? Basically, Korea was a mountainous peninsula jutting south from the Asian land mass, a

1–5 The rugged terrain of Korea.

1–6 The unforgiving Korean winter.

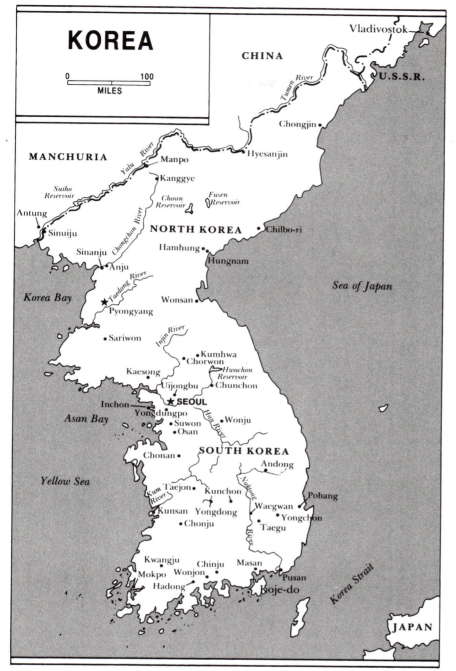

Map 1 The Korean Peninsula

600-mile–long piece of land, some 85,000 square miles, about the size of Utah, and more or less shaped like Florida. It extended through nine parallels of latitude, from the 43d to the 34th (in the United States, roughly from Boston, Massachusetts, to Columbia, South Carolina). The 38th Parallel, about the latitude of Lexington, Kentucky, was the political North-South border. In width, Korea varied from 200 miles at the broadest point to 90 miles at its narrow waist. Much of the land was mountainous, with the dominant feature being the Taebaek Range, which ran down the east coast like an ugly spine and caused most of Korea's rivers to flow westward.

On the west, accepting those waters, was the Yellow Sea, beyond which lay China. To the east, the Sea of Japan separated Korea from the Japanese homelands, the "Land of the Rising Sun." To the south was the Korea Strait. Korea's east coast had almost no tide. In the west, however, the tides were considerable, and, at Inchon, the tidal reach of 32 feet was the second highest in the world.

On the north was Korea's only land border, marked by the Yalu and Tumen Rivers. On the far shore of those rivers was a 500-mile stretch of Chinese Manchuria and, at the northeastern tip of the Korean peninsula, a small, 11-mile section of Soviet Siberia. That tip was within 90 miles of Vladivostok, a port city whose name, chosen by the Czars, means *Dominion of the East.*

The "Land of the Morning Calm" **3**

1–7 The battleship USS *Wisconsin* patrolling Korean waters.

1–8 Buddhist shrine.

1–9 Father Charles Meeus saying Mass for Korean children.

The fact that Korea was almost completely surrounded by water had strategic importance, for the U.S. Navy's control of those waters would be a significant factor during the Korean War (1–7). Unlike Vietnam, half of which has land boundaries and where it became almost impossible to contain infiltration, entry to Korea could come only from one direction—the north.

Korea's 1950 population was about thirty million. North Korea, although it contained 60 percent of the land area, had less than one third of the population, or about nine million. The people mainly practiced either Buddhism or Confucianism, with shrines like the one in photograph 1–8 scattered throughout the land. There was also a small percentage of Christians; photograph 1–9 shows Father Charles Meeus, a Belgian missionary priest, saying Mass for Korean children. Because the North generated most of the peninsula's electricity, it owned the bulk of Korean heavy industry. South Korea, on the other hand, having few manufacturing facilities, was almost entirely agricultural, with rice and barley the main crops. Whether north or south, however, farmers made do with what they had. Only 20 percent of the land was arable, but every little piece of ground, such as the one in photograph 1–10, was terraced, irrigated, and cultivated.

1–10 Paddy field in built-up area.

1–11 Farmer and his primitive ox-drawn cart. The banner in the background is in Japanese, which illustrates the remaining Japanese influence in Korea.

Communication and transportation were primitive (1–11). The entire country had fewer than 50 miles of paved roads. Otherwise, even the main thoroughfares were merely surfaces of improved gravel (1–12). Under any kind of heavy traffic, that meant mud in the summer and dust in the winter. In the north, there were several single-track rail lines; in the south, the country's only double-track rail line ran from the capital, Seoul, southeast to Pusan, the major port on the east coast.

In the countryside, where most of the people lived, Korean homes were one-story buildings made of mud and small sticks (1–13) with wooden rafters supporting thatched roofs. At one end of the house was the kitchen, whose fire kept the house warm in winter through a "chimney" that ran under the floor of the house and up the outside wall at the other end of the house. A low wall often connected the house to two outlying sheds, one for animals and the other for the family toilet. The house had no running water or electricity.

In addition to Land of the Morning Calm, Korea has another

1–12 Farmer on unpaved thoroughfare.

1–13 Typical Korean home.

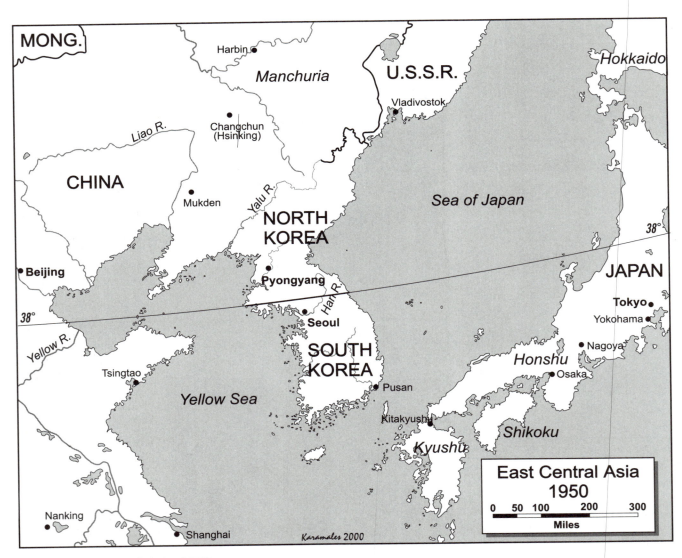

Map 2 East Central Asia, 1950

traditional nickname: "The Hermit Kingdom." For centuries, Korean rulers did their best to remain isolated and clear of great-power politics. They were seldom successful, for it was Korea's fortune—or misfortune—to be located where the spheres of three great powers, Russia, China, and Japan, came together. Even had they wanted, those powers could not have ignored the Korean peninsula and its strategic location. Since ancient times, Korea has been the invasion route of Japan into the Asian continent, as well as the dagger aimed at Japan from Asia. An old Korean maxim says, "When whales collide, the shrimp in the middle is the one who suffers." Sadly, that often has been the fate of Korea—the "shrimp in the middle"—feeling pain as its neighbors collide.

Korea has an ancient civilization, one in which its people take justifiable pride. Its written history dates from the time of Christ, and ancient historic tombs, monuments, and temples, such as the one in photograph 1–14, are scattered throughout the country. Unlike other Oriental cultures, Koreans have their own phonetic Hangul alphabet; one developed more than five hundred years ago. They were also pioneers in the use of movable metal type. The first authenticated casting occurred in

1403, which predated Gutenberg by fifty years, and Korea long led the world in the development of the printing art.

Understandably, much of Korea's history is interwoven with that of China. As early as the second century, Chinese colonists began to influence Korea's agriculture, writing system, and its ideas of religion and statecraft. By the seventh century, Korea's Silla Dynasty, with the capital at Kyongju, had established a strong provincial administration and land system along Chinese lines. The Hermit Kingdom, however, would not be left alone, as attacks from a series of foreign foes, notably the Mongols, continued. For long periods, with the Mongols' fierce horsemen ravaging the countryside, Korea was little more than an appendage of the Mongol empire. The Silla Dynasty gave way to the Koryo Dynasty, which also fell, after centuries of unrest, through the efforts of a legendary Korean strongman, Gen. Yi Song-gye. Photograph 1–15 shows the famed South Gate of Seoul built during the Koryo Dynasty. The ensuing Yi Dynasty (1392–1910) was one of the longest continuous regimes in the history of mankind.

In 1592, after two centuries of almost unbroken peace, Korea was invaded by a ruthless Japanese leader, Hideyoshi. His well-armed warriors landed at Pusan, quickly cut through Korea's defenders, and advanced as far as Pyongyang. When Hideyoshi paused to regroup, the Koreans

1–14 Historic pagoda.

1–15 South gate of Seoul.

1–16 Statue of Adm. Yi Sun-sin, Korean naval hero.

1–17 Shinto shrine where students studied.

sought aid from China and rallied the people to a historic resistance. Meanwhile, the great Korean hero, Adm. Yi Sun-sin, defeated the Japanese at sea with his famed "turtle ship," the world's first armored vessel (1–16). Eventually, with help from China, the Koreans expelled the Japanese from the peninsula.

More incursions were to follow, both from China and Japan. Finally, following yet another Japanese invasion during the late nineteenth century, Korea again sought Chinese help. The resulting Sino-Japanese War, a brief, one-sided struggle, ended in a quick victory for Japan. In 1895, under the Treaty of Shimonoseki, Japan was left in substantial control of the Korean government. This not only ended Chinese political influence in Korea but also brought Russia onto the scene. Almost predictably, Russian ambitions in Manchuria clashed with Japanese plans for Korea. This resulted in the Russo-Japanese War of 1904–1905, begun when the Japanese, without declaring war (in an eerie foreshadowing of Pearl Harbor and that "day of infamy," December 7, 1941), attacked the Russian fleet at Port Arthur. Once again, there was a quick Japanese victory. The Treaty of Portsmouth, intermediated by American President Theodore Roosevelt, left Japan dominant in Korea.

Step by step, despite the resentment and bitter opposition of the Korean people, Japan methodically absorbed Korea into the Japanese empire. Finally, in 1910, Japan annexed Korea as a colony. For the next thirty-five years, the Japanese masters ruled with an iron hand. In 1919, for example, when unarmed demonstrators took to the streets after their leaders published an eloquent "declaration of independence," thousands of Koreans were arrested and hundreds were killed. During the years that followed, Japanese dominance became all-pervasive. The native Korean language was banned; Koreans were made to adopt Japanese names; and Korean schoolchildren were forced to do obeisance at Shinto shrines, such as the one shown in photograph 1–17. The Japanese held all supervisory and managerial positions in the government, the police, and the factories, and they restricted the native Koreans to clerical positions.

1–18 Two outlets of underground petroleum tanks built by the Japanese to refuel their battleships during World War II.

Although this period of Japanese rule (1910–1945) brought considerable economic growth to Korea, the benefits accrued primarily to the Japanese (1–18). Understandably, these oppressive measures made the Korean people yearn for more freedom. The slightest hint of resistance, however, was punished by imprisonment or worse. Nevertheless, the Koreans continued to struggle for independence. For good reason, they are called "the Irish of the Orient."

During World War II, many Koreans organized partisan bands and battled the Japanese in both Manchuria and China. All Koreans, especially these freedom fighters, were thrilled by the Allies' Cairo Declaration of 1943, by which the United States, Great Britain, and China promised that "in due course, Korea shall become free and independent" (1–19).

1–19 Franklin D. Roosevelt of the United States, Ismet Inonu of Turkey, and Winston Churchill of Great Britain, at the 1943 Cairo conference.

1–20 Gen. Douglas MacArthur with his trademark, a corncob pipe.

not land in Korea until September 8, and it was September 9 before they reached Seoul. Korea was now occupied militarily by two foreign nations with separate and conflicting agendas.

Unfortunately, it proved almost impossible for the Americans to work in harmony with the Soviets. A U.S.-Soviet wartime alliance had been forged because of a common enemy, Nazi Germany. Now that the Nazi threat had been removed, the main reason for that alliance no longer existed. Joint U.S.-Soviet commissions met in Seoul in March 1946 to work out the details of a provisional government but failed to reach an agreement (1–21). A second round of joint commission meetings took place in 1947, but they also met the brick wall of Soviet intransigence (1–22). Finally, in September 1947, the

In August of 1945, after the dropping of atomic bombs on Hiroshima and Nagasaki, the Japanese surrender, presided over by Gen. Douglas MacArthur on the battleship *Missouri*, brought an end to World War II (1–20). The Soviet Union had also subscribed to the Cairo Declaration and had declared war on Japan only a few days prior to its surrender. Nevertheless, the Soviet Union became a full partner in the surrender ceremonies. The parties agreed that the United States and the Soviet Union would divide Korea into North and South zones of responsibility for receiving the surrender of Japanese troops. They further agreed, almost casually, that, as a matter of convenience, the 38th Parallel of latitude would be the line of demarcation.

Soviet soldiers swarmed out of Manchuria. By August 26 they

had reached the 38th Parallel and sealed off the demarcation line. By that date, the Americans heading for Korea were just beginning to board ships in Okinawa. They did

1–21 Meeting in Seoul between U.S. and USSR commissions in March 1946. (Seated, left to right, Lt. Gen. John R. Hodge, Col. General D. F. Stikoff, and Maj. Gen. N. G. Lebedoff.)

1–22 The Military Armistice Commission in 1947. Maj. Gen. Hobart Hewitt, commission chief of staff, is in front row, center.

United Nations (UN) General Assembly adopted a resolution providing for Korea-wide elections under UN supervision. After Soviet authorities refused to permit UN representatives to enter North Korea, elections were held in South Korea alone. In other words, Korea-wide reunification was no longer in the cards. This came as a bitter pill to Korean elder statesman Syngman Rhee (1–23). At the end of World War II, Rhee had criticized the United States and its Allies for the de facto division of Korea at the 38th Parallel. Now that division was being cast in stone.

Many Koreans regarded Syngman Rhee as their George Wash-

1–23 Syngman Rhee reviews the troops.

1–24 Seoul, Korea, 1950.

1–25 Kim Il Sung, communist leader of North Korea.

paigned tirelessly for a united and independent Korea.

On August 15, 1948, the U.S. military government in South Korea was terminated, and, in Seoul (1–24), with Syngman Rhee as its first president, the Republic of Korea (ROK) was formally proclaimed. The following month in the North, hard-line communists chosen by the Soviet Union established the Democratic People's Republic of Korea under President Kim Il Sung.

Kim Il Sung, known in later years as North Korea's "Great Leader," was born in 1912 in the town of Mangyongdae, near North Korea's capital city, Pyongyang (1–25). His early history is unclear, but he and his family supposedly left Korea for Manchuria to escape the Japanese occupation. In 1926, he joined China's Communist Youth League and later attended the Whampoa Military Academy in Canton. According to his official biography, he traveled to the Soviet Union during World War II, studied at a Russian military academy, and later commanded one of the two Korean units that fought at Stalingrad. By war's end, he had risen to the rank of lieutenant colonel and had been awarded the Order of Lenin by Soviet Premier Joseph Stalin (1–26). When Soviet troops entered Korea in August 1945, they brought Kim with them to administer the country.

ington. He was born in 1875 in what is now North Korea and became an active member of the Korean student movement. In 1897, he was jailed and tortured. Rhee converted to Christianity while in jail. After his release in 1904, he came to the United States, where he received a B.A. from George Washington University, an M.A. from Harvard University, and a Ph.D. in theology from Princeton University.

When Rhee returned to Korea in 1910, he again participated in revolutionary activity and was forced by the Japanese to flee the country. He became an active leader of a Korean provisional government in exile and cam-

By now, he had been promoted to general in recognition of his guerrilla activities in Manchuria. It appears, however, that in true Communist fashion, much of his military background was either imaginary or greatly inflated and carefully tailored to suit communist needs. The Japanese authorities, until 1945, described Kim Il Sung as a bandit chieftain of about forty to fifty marauders. The "division" he allegedly commanded in the Chinese Route Army was only about three hundred men strong, and, although he probably did serve in the Soviet Army as a colonel during World War II, he returned to Pyongyang not as a colonel but as a Soviet Army major.

In the North, President Kim Il Sung, the self-proclaimed "Great Leader," was appointed supreme commander of the North Korean People's Army (NKPA). With help from the Soviets, including a large infusion of equipment, he began to build this army into a potent force.

Meanwhile, in the South, a small number of Americans known as the Korean Military Advisory Group (KMAG) remained to help build from scratch a new ROK Army. By June 1949, all other American military personnel had pulled out. As shown in photograph 1–27, they were happy to be headed home.

1–26 Joseph Stalin, shown here on Moscow reviewing stand with Marshal Kliment Voroshilov, was instrumental in Kim Il Sung's becoming North Korean president.

1–27 American personnel happily departing Korea in June 1949. Little did they know that U.S. troops would soon return.

⊢TWO⊣

Prelude to War

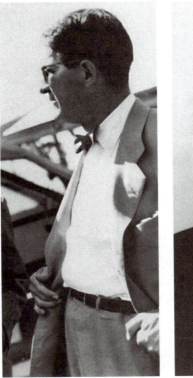

2–1 John J. Muccio, U.S. Ambassador to Korea.

2–2 Kim Il Sung.

2–3 Syngman Rhee.

When American occupation troops began leaving Korea, Syngman Rhee, the South's strong-willed president, had already established himself as a dominant force, fully supported (but with some misgivings) by the American authorities, including Ambassador John J. Muccio (2–1).

In the North, Kim Il Sung (2–2) was likewise strengthening his position, casting noncommunists out of the government, and using his close ties with the Soviets, plus his reputation as a guerrilla leader, to solidify his support.

Although the regimes in both the North and the South were now clearly in power, they faced similar challenges. For each of them, the existence of the other state was an irritating obstacle to full legitimacy. Predictably, Syngman Rhee (2–3) made the claim that *his* regime was the only legal government on the peninsula. In the north, Kim Il Sung was saying the same thing. Understandably, the two leaders were soon denouncing each other and calling for a crusade to unify the country under their own respective authorities.

In Japan, meanwhile, the American occupation was becoming one of the marvels of the twentieth century. Never before had a victor done so much to rebuild a former enemy country nor to transform its very culture. Gen. Douglas MacArthur, Supreme Commander Allied Powers (SCAP) (2–4), from his headquarters in Tokyo's Dai Ichi Building (2–5), had become an awesome figure to the Japanese. Reforms pushed by MacArthur, but carried out by the Japanese themselves, gave women the vote, encouraged the "unionization of labor," liberalized schools toward the teaching of democracy, ended monopolies, and ensured public ownership of production and trade. Under MacArthur's guidance, moreover, the Japanese proceeded to write a new, democratic constitution. As the *New York Times* reported: "Japan is the one bright spot in Allied military government. General MacArthur's administration is a model of government and a boon to peace in the Far East. He has swept away an autocratic regime by a warrior god and installed in its place a democratic government presided over by a very human emperor and based on the will of the people as expressed in free elections."

The U.S. armed forces in Japan, however, were not nearly so impressive. Following the end of World War II, America's military had been cut to the bone. In 1945, the United States had spent $50 billion on its army; in 1950 it spent $5 billion. In 1945, there were 8,250,000 men on active service; in 1950, there were less than 600,000. The American people, gripped by peacetime euphoria and anxious to "get the boys home" quickly, had not complained.

The U.S. Eighth Army in Japan, under Lt. Gen. Walton H. Walker (2–6), had four divisions.

2–4 Gen. Douglas MacArthur, Supreme Commander Allied Powers (left), salutes as he leaves his headquarters in Tokyo.

2–5 The roof of the Dai Ichi Building in Tokyo, MacArthur's headquarters. Note the U.S., UN, and Japanese flags flying side by side.

2–6 Lt. Gen. Walton H. Walker, Commander, U.S. Eighth Army.

2–7 Lt. Gen. George E. Stratemeyer, Commander, Far East Air Force.

2–9 F-51 Mustang, said to be the best prop fighter ever built.

2–10 F-80 Shooting Star, America's first jet fighter.

2–8 Maj. Gen. Earle E. Partridge, Commander, Fifth Air Force.

The sixty-year–old Walker, who had distinguished himself during World War II as one of Gen. George S. Patton's corps commanders, did the best he could with what he had. Because of peacetime economies, however, the Eighth was really a "hollow" army. The divisions had two regiments instead of the standard three, the regiments had two battalions instead of three, the artillery battalions had two firing batteries instead of three, and so on. Moreover, as one veteran recalled, "we were using equipment and weapons salvaged from Okinawa and places like that. We never saw anything *new*."

Nevertheless, morale was reasonably high. Athletic teams, service clubs, USO shows, PX supplies, servants for those whose dependents had arrived, and, for those so inclined, a smiling Japanese girlfriend (*musuma*) were available. All in all, occupation duty was rather pleasant. Whereas the troops were not "fat and lazy," as some historians later said, they were nevertheless far from combat ready.

Although the Far East Air Force, under Lt. Gen. George E. Stratemeyer (2–7), and the U.S. Fifth Air Force, under Maj. Gen. Earle E. Partridge (2–8), were in better shape than the Army, they too were well below authorized strength. Stratemeyer had nine wings, or thirty squadrons, under his control, a total of 1,172 aircraft. Of these, however, only 553 were in operational combat units; the rest were in storage or in repair depots, or they were used for training, transport, or liaison. Stratemeyer was espe-

2–11 B-29 Superfortress preparing to take off.

cially short of what he most needed, attack and ground-support aircraft—F-51 Mustangs (2–9) and F-80 Shooting Star jet fighters (2–10). To supplement them, he had 26 B-26 light bombers and 22 B-29 Superfortresses (2–11). Base maintenance and communication facilities were just barely adequate.

The U.S. Navy in the Far East was probably in the best shape of any of the services. Naval forces in the Pacific were under the command of Adm. Arthur W. Radford (2–12); U.S. Naval Forces Far East were commanded by Vice Adm. C. Turner Joy (2–13). In nearby waters, the Navy had a cruiser, a destroyer division, part of a minesweeper squadron, and a small amphibious force. To the south, although not under MacArthur's command, was the Seventh Fleet, commanded by Vice Adm. Arthur D. Struble (2–14) and comprised of the aircraft carrier *Valley Forge*, a heavy cruiser, and eight destroyers. The Navy's presence, and command of the seas, would turn out to be a crucial factor in the war that lay just over the horizon.

2–12 Adm. Arthur W. Radford, Commander, U.S. Naval Forces Far East.

2–13 Vice Adm. C. Turner Joy, Commander, Far East Naval Forces.

2–14 Vice Adm. Arthur D. Struble, Commander, Seventh Fleet.

During the late 1940s, with U.S. forces leaving Korea and conditions generally under control in Japan, the United States had been turning its attention more and more toward a troubled Europe. In 1945, the "Big Three," Truman, Churchill, and Stalin, met at Potsdam, Germany (2–15). In 1946, Winston Churchill delivered his "Iron Curtain" speech and gave a new term to the Cold War vocabulary. As Soviet hostility continued, President Harry S Truman had proclaimed the "Truman Doctrine," announcing America's intent to contain the spread of international communism. In June 1947, U.S. Secretary of State George C. Marshall (2–16) announced the economic recovery plan bearing his name, one designed to create a more stable world. Then, in June of 1948, as American withdrawal from Korea was well under way, the Soviet Union instituted its infamous Berlin Blockade, countered by the historic U.S. airlift that lasted for nearly a year until the Soviets lifted the siege. In April of 1949, the North American Treaty Organization (NATO) was formed, with U.S. Gen. Dwight D. Eisenhower named as its first commander (2–17). In July of that year, the Soviets exploded their first atomic bomb, which showed that America's technological lead was far shorter than had been hoped. Understandably, Europe was getting most of the attention. By the end of 1949, not only NATO Commander Eisenhower but also the Truman Administration and the U.S. Joint Chiefs of Staff were focusing on Europe.

2–15 Left to right, Soviet Premier Joseph Stalin, President Harry S Truman, and Prime Minister Winston Churchill at Potsdam, 1945.

2–16 George C. Marshall, U.S. Secretary of State.

In January of 1949, the aristocratic Dean Acheson replaced the ailing George Marshall as U.S. Secretary of State (2–18). Acheson was a dedicated, even brilliant, public servant, but his public and congressional relations were hurt by his professional demeanor and his haughty disregard for those he considered his intellectual inferiors. As 1950 began, Korea could not have been high on Acheson's list of "Where the Balloon May Go Up" during the coming year. Iran, Greece, and Middle Europe were more likely locales for Soviet troublemaking. Acheson was also concerned about the coming Japanese treaty, the newly established NATO, and the possibility of communists being voted to power in either Italy or France.

In any event, when Acheson spoke to the National Press Club in January of 1950, his remarks about American defense interests in Asia proved both significant and unfortunate. America's "defensive perimeter," Acheson said, "runs along the Aleutians to Japan and then goes to the Ryukyus . . . from the Ryukyus to the Philippine Islands." Korea was not included in this perimeter nor were the forces of Generalissimo Chiang Kai-shek on Formosa. They were among "other areas" in the Pacific and, said Acheson, "no person can guarantee these areas against military attack." To the communist world, this might have seemed like a green light. Presumably, if Korea were attacked, America would remain on the sidelines.

2–17 Gen. Dwight D. Eisenhower (sitting, center), meeting with NATO Standing Group Officers.

The North Korean People's Army

As early as 1946, Russia had begun building a North Korean military capability, not only by providing arms but by establishing training centers using Soviet troops. North Korean Labor Party members were urged to enlist as were those with previous military service as guerrillas or as members of the Japanese army. There was also a general conscription of men between the ages of eighteen and thirty-five; however, the North Korean government did not announce the activation of an armed force under the title "People's Army" until February 8, 1948. The overall strength of the North Korean People's Army at the time was about 30,000. In addition, there were about

2–18 Dean Acheson, Marshall's replacement, in January 1949.

2–19 Soviet-built T-34 tank—dominant weapon of the war's early days.

2–20 ROK soldiers engaged in mortar training.

2–21 ROK marines in training.

170,000 trainees, including members of the Police Constabulary.

By June of 1950, on the eve of the Korean War, the NKPA (*In Mun Gun*) had between 150,000 and 180,000 men. It had approximately 150 Soviet-made T-34 tanks (2–19), and three types of artillery, 122-mm howitzers, 76-mm self-propelled guns, and about 150 aircraft, with pilots, aircraft mechanics, tankers, and tank maintenance personnel all having been trained by the Soviets.

The Republic of Korea Armed Forces

In the South, the army had evolved from what was initially a constabulary force. In October of 1948, this new force was put to the test by an internal revolt that broke out at Yosu. Loyal constabulary troops rushed to the scene and, after several days of savage fighting, managed to quell the communist-inspired rebellion. As a result of the Yosu revolt, some 1,500 communists were purged from the constabulary.

In December of 1948, the ROK government set up the Departments of National Defense, Army, and Navy. At the same time, all constabulary forces became part of the ROK Army. By June of 1950, the ROK Army was organized into eight combat divisions totaling approximately 65,000 men. They were equipped with the U.S. M-1 rifle, .30-caliber carbine, and 60-mm and 81-mm mortars. Photograph 2–20 shows young ROK soldiers engaged in mortar training. Other American

2–22 ROK sailors performing calisthenics.

2–23 ROK sailors rowing during basic training.

weapons included 2.36-inch rocket launchers, 37-mm anti-tank guns, and 105-mm how-itzers. As a matter of policy, how-ever, the United States did not want South Korea to be capable of waging aggressive warfare. Consequently the South Korean armed forces received no tanks, medium artillery, 4.2-inch mor-tars, recoilless rifles, fighter air-craft, or bombers. Similarly, the ROK Navy consisted only of a patrol craft recently purchased from the United States, three other similar craft at Hawaii en route to Korea, one landing ship, tank (LST), fifteen former U.S. minesweepers, ten former Japan-ese minelayers, and various other small craft. Despite the shortages of equipment, ROK marines and sailors trained with enthusiasm, as shown in photographs 2–21, 2–22, and 2–23.

The KMAG consisted of five hundred American advisors provided to assist the South Korean military. Scattered throughout South Korea, they worked hard to build the ROK armed forces.

Prelude

Early in 1950, Kim Il Sung began to plan a full-scale attack on South Korea with the goal of uni-fying the country through military force. Before launching such an attack, however, he needed the approval of Joseph Stalin, who if not his "master," was at least the man supplying the tools of war. He also needed an okay from Chinese Chairman Mao Tse-tung

2–24 Chairman Mao Tse-tung of the People's Republic of China.

(2–24). After persistent appeals by Kim and a go-ahead from Mao, Stalin gave his reluctant approval for the attack after making sure that sufficient arms and equipment were on hand to provide significant military superiority. He also sent Soviet military advisors to Korea to help plan the campaign. From the most recent evidence, it appears that Kim assured Stalin of a quick military victory, one that would include a communist-led general uprising against the controversial Syngman Rhee (2–25). Moreover, it seems clear that Kim never believed that the United States would intervene.

On the night of June 24, Soviet howitzers and self-propelled guns were already positioned along the 38th Parallel. Some 150 Soviet-made T-34 tanks were cautiously moving forward to their attack positions, along with ninety thousand Soviet-trained combat troops. The stage was set. The curtain was about to rise on a brutal, bloody war.

2–25 Syngman Rhee (left), controversial president of South Korea, talking with U.S. Vice President Alben W. Barkley.

⊣THREE⊢
South to the Naktong

3–1 Seoul, looking east from the Banta Hotel.

Early on Sunday morning, June 25, 1950, North Korean forces stormed across the 38th Parallel in a fierce, well-coordinated attack that stunned both the South Korean defenders and their American advisors. In the South Korean capital of Seoul (3–1), panicky civilians clamored for information (3–2, 3–3). For a time, the ROK Army, said to be counterattacking, appeared to have the situation contained. It soon became evident, however, that, after a brave initial resistance, the South Koreans were being overwhelmed. U.S. Ambassador John J. Muccio fired off a cable to get Washington stirring: "It would appear from the nature of the attack and the manner it was launched, that it constitutes an all-out offensive against the Republic of Korea."

3–2 Korean citizens crowd the entrances of City Hall as they await war news.

3–3 Refugees panicking as hostilities unfold.

President Truman, who had gone home to Missouri for the weekend, hurried back to the capital (3–4). After meeting with his national security advisors, he had U.S. Ambassador Warren Austin, recommend to the UN Security Council that "Members of the United Nations furnish such assistance to the Republic of Korea as may be necessary to repel the armed attack and to restore international peace and security in the area." In London, Prime Minister Clement Attlee read Truman's resolution to the House of Commons. The North Korean attack, Attlee said, "is naked aggression and must be stopped." He said the British representative at the Security Council had been instructed to support the American resolution. Fortunately for the United States, Jacob Malik, the

3–4 President Harry S Truman.

3–5 Jacob Malik, Soviet representative to the UN Security Council.

3–6 Devastated South Korean town.

Soviet representative, was boycotting the Security Council at the time in protest of the fact that Communist China had not been given a seat (3–5). The Soviets had outsmarted themselves. With Malik absenting himself from the meeting, where he could have exercised a veto, the motion was carried.

Meanwhile, some ninety thousand North Koreans, equipped with Soviet weapons and Soviet T-34 tanks, were brushing aside South Korean defenses and moving forward relentlessly as they left devastated towns in their wake (3–6). Within two days, communist forces had captured Uijongbu, a highway center 20 miles north of Seoul. As dispirited South Korean soldiers began moving south (3–7), Americans and other foreign nationals were being evacuated (3–8, 3–9). The attack rolled on, and by Wednesday, June 28, Seoul had fallen to the North Koreans. Early that morning, the main bridges over the Han River had been blown up by ROK Army engineers with no warning to the military personnel and civilian refugees crowding the bridges. Not only were hundreds killed, the ROKs, by destroying the bridges prematurely, had also trapped forty-four thousand of their own men north of the river.

On orders from President Truman, carrier-based planes of the U.S. Navy and Marines (3–10 to 3–13) and Air Force fighters,

3–7 South Korean soldiers retreating from Seoul.

3–9 U.S. Army captain speaking to three nuns at a railway station somewhere in Korea during the early days of the communist invasion.

3–8 Americans (probably members of the Korean Military Advisory Group) evacuating Seoul.

3–10 U.S. Navy F-9 Panthers prepare to take off from a carrier. This was the first time in naval history that jet aircraft were used in combat.

3–11 U.S. Navy Panthers flying a sortie.

3–12 USS *Badoeng Strait* nearing Japan with F-4U Corsairs on board.

including F-51 Mustangs and F-80 Shooting Stars, began to fly missions in support of the South Koreans (3–14 to 3–17). Some of the results are shown in photographs 3–18, 3–19, and 3–20. Truman also ordered the U.S. Seventh Fleet to the Taiwan Strait to protect Formosa. In Japan, Douglas MacArthur decided to see the situation for himself. "The only way to judge a fight is to see the troops in action," he told his staff. On June 29, MacArthur, taking off from Tokyo's Haneda Airport, headed for Korea in his personal plane, the *Bataan*, along with Maj. Gen. Edward M. ("Ned") Almond, his chief of staff; Maj. Gen. E. K. Wright, his operations officer; and

3–13 F-4U Corsair armed with 8 rockets and a 500-pound bomb takes off from the USS *Sicily*.

3–14 Sgt. Dewey Lukefahr of Perryville, Missouri, anchors a 500-pound bomb to the wing of a plane.

3–15 Fifty-caliber ammunition being loaded into an F-51 Mustang at an airfield in South Korea.

3–16 Airman loading rockets onto an F-51 Mustang. (Note the name painted on the fuselage of the aircraft.)

3–17 Airman working on the Rolls-Royce engine of an F-51 Mustang.

3–18 Locomotive knocked out by U.S. Air Force planes lies on its side near the Han River in Korea.

3–19 An enemy tank destroyed by an F-80 with two five-inch rockets.

Lt. Gen. George E. Stratemeyer, his air chief. MacArthur was shocked by what he found. The situation was chaotic, with streams of refugees flowing south and shattered ROK Army units unable to form a solid defensive line. Although one ROK division was digging in along the line of the Han, it was clear that the division could not hold its position (3–21 to 3–24).

MacArthur's report to Washington described the ROK Army's

3–20 Two probable direct hits on railroad bridges over the Kum River, 10 miles north of Taejon.

great loss of personnel and equipment and said that everything possible was being done to maintain a flow of supplies from Japan (3–25, 3–26). He knew, however, that the ROK Army desperately needed help. "The only assurance for the holding of the present line, and the ability to regain later the lost ground," MacArthur told the Joint Chiefs, "is through the introduction of U.S. ground combat forces into the Korean battle area. To continue to utilize the forces of our Air and Navy without an effective ground element cannot be decisive." He urged the immediate deployment of an American regimental combat team, followed by a further buildup from Eighth Army divisions presently in Japan.

President Truman met with State and Defense officials and approved the sending of two divisions to Korea from Japan and

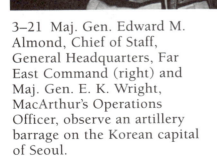

3–21 Maj. Gen. Edward M. Almond, Chief of Staff, General Headquarters, Far East Command (right) and Maj. Gen. E. K. Wright, MacArthur's Operations Officer, observe an artillery barrage on the Korean capital of Seoul.

3–22 Gen. Douglas MacArthur (at right) greets Lt. Gen. Walton H. Walker.

3–23 MacArthur (center) with his chief of staff, General Almond (right), and Ambassador John J. Muccio.

3–24 MacArthur at Yongdung-po, June 29, 1950.

3–25 UN weapons arrive at Pusan.

3–26 UN weapons arrive at Pusan.

establishing a naval blockade of North Korea. At a press conference, Truman was asked if the country was at war.

"No, we are not at war," he replied.

"Would it be possible to call this a police action under the United Nations?" a reporter asked.

"Yes, that is exactly what it amounts to," Truman said, "a police action taken to help the UN repel a bunch of bandits." Later,

American GIs would quote the term *police action* with grim irony.

Following passage of the Security Council resolution, the United Nations Command was established, with Douglas MacArthur as its first commander. General Headquarters, Far East Command, then became the principal part of General Headquarters, United Nations Command (GHQ UNC). Other nations were asked to lend all possible support. MacArthur,

wanting to establish an American presence quickly, ordered Lt. Gen. Walton H. Walker, Commander, Eighth Army, to dispatch a reinforced battalion combat team to Korea without delay. Unfortunately, in the understrength Eighth Army, no such battalion force existed; it would have to be cobbled together. Walker called on Maj. Gen. William F. ("Bill") Dean (3–27), Commander, 24th Infantry Division, the force headquartered

3–27 Maj. Gen. William F. Dean, Commander, 24th Infantry Division.

3–29 A C-54 Skymaster in Korea.

3–28 Brig. Gen. John Church, commander of an advance unit (shown here after promotion to general).

closest to Korea. Dean, in turn, gave the mission to Col. Richard W. ("Big Six") Stephens, the forty-seven-year-old, barrel-chested, aggressive commander of the Gimlets, the 21st Infantry Regiment.

Task Force Smith

Late on the night of June 30, Stephens called Lt. Col. Brad Smith, commander of the regiment's 1st Battalion. "The lid has blown off," Stephens said, "get on your clothes and report to the CP [command post]!" When the thirty-four-year-old Smith arrived at the CP, Stephens told him to prepare Rifle Companies B and C from his battalion for immediate movement to Itazuke Air Base. Stephens would grab men from other units to bring those rifle companies up to strength; he would also beef up Smith with some heavy weapons, plus a communications section and a medical section. In addition, a detachment from the 52d Field Artillery Battalion would link up with them in Korea.

Early next morning, when the newly created Task Force Smith arrived at Itazuke, its crew-cut division commander, fifty-year-old Bill Dean, was on hand to meet them. "When you get to Pusan," Dean told Smith, "head for Taejon. We want to stop the North Koreans as far from Pusan as we can. Block the main road as far north as possible. Contact General Church [Brig. Gen. John Church, already on the ground as head of an advance unit, 3–28]. If you can't locate him, go to Taejon and beyond if you can. Sorry I can't give you more information, but that's all I've got. Good luck to you and God bless you and your men."

The task force was shuttled in Air Force C-54 Skymasters, tired but sturdy veterans of World War II (3–29), to an airfield near Pusan at the southeastern tip of the Korean Peninsula. Eventually,

3–30 Townspeople welcoming UN troops at Kumchon, June 30, 1950.

3–31 Banner welcoming U.S. Army to Kumchon.

3–32 Refugees fleeing south as the task force prepares to move north toward the front.

the heavily loaded Skymasters tore up the dirt airstrip, which curtailed the airlift, cut Smith's heavy firepower in half, and reduced his force from 440 to 406 men. As the Americans traveled in various commandeered vehicles to the Pusan rail station, cheering crowds lined the streets and waved banners, flags, and streamers. Photographs 3–30 and 3–31, taken when Americans arrived at Kumchon, show a similar welcoming demonstration. That evening at the rail yard, a Korean band, on hand to give Smith's men a noisy sendoff, created almost a holiday atmosphere. The mood was dampened, however, when a train loaded with South Korean casualties pulled in on an adjacent siding. "My God," someone said, "maybe there's a real war on!" Overall, however, there was a general feeling of confidence, a belief that the North Koreans would back off once they realized that the Americans had entered the fight.

Arriving at Taejon, Smith met with General Church, who said, "We have a little action up here. All we need are some men who won't run when they see tanks. We're going to move you up to support the ROKs and give them moral support." It wasn't much of a briefing nor was it very realistic, but it was all the briefing Smith was going to get. Pushing its way through swarms of refugees, similar to those shown in photograph 3–32, the task force headed north.

3–33 A highly feared T-34 tank with its 85-mm main gun.

3–34 105-mm howitzer in operation.

Smith selected a good defensive position just north of Osan, a place where the main highway ran through a saddle and descended into a long valley. He deployed his men on low hills astride the road; from these, they could see all the way to Suwon, eight miles to the northwest, and could cover by fire both the highway and a nearby rail line. Early on the morning of July 5, Smith looked through his binoculars and saw in the distance a column of thirty-three tanks—Soviet-supplied T-34s mounting powerful 85-mm cannons (3–33). The tanks were coming south in single file and unescorted by infantry, which meant that they expected no opposition. They would have made great targets for aerial rockets, but the day was overcast and no planes were flying. Antitank mines also would have helped, but Smith had been told that they were unavailable. Therefore, the Americans would have to rely on their 105-mm artillery (3–34), recoilless rifles, and bazookas (hand-held 2.36-inch rocket launchers).

When the tanks came within range, however, the Americans found to their dismay that none of their ordnance—recoilless rifle shells, bazooka rounds, or artillery high explosives—could penetrate the T-34s' thick armor. (Artillery HEAT [high explosive antitank] rounds *could* penetrate, but there were only six HEAT rounds on hand, one third of the entire division supply.)

Seemingly indifferent to the exploding shells, the tanks rolled on. They soon began blasting away at the American positions with their cannons and machine guns. The lone American antitank howitzer disabled two of the tanks. The third tank coming through the pass put the howitzer out of action with a single round from its 85-mm main gun, but all six of the howitzer's antitank rounds already had been fired. As the tanks advanced, their tracks tore up the telephone wire laid alongside the road, thus destroying any landline communication with the rear. "It was heartbreaking," recalled one young lieutenant, "to watch those men firing point-blank and doing little damage. Rockets hit the tanks in the tracks, turrets, and bogies [wheels], and still they couldn't stop them!"

In frustration, the Americans watched the tanks roll on to the south. About 11 A.M., after a momentary lull, Smith spotted more movement on the road to his front. Three enemy tanks were leading a column of trucks. On board the trucks were two NKPA regiments, between four thousand and five thousand men. When the lead trucks came within 1,000 yards of the infantry position, Task Force Smith opened up with everything it had. The mortars and machine guns were especially effective. Trucks burst into flames; men were blown into the air or jumped from the vehicles into roadside ditches. The enemy column came to an abrupt halt, and soon crowds of infantry began to deploy. By 2:30 P.M., with ammunition running low and the enemy established on both flanks, Smith

3–35 Task Force Smith veterans being honored by President Truman at the White House in June 1952. Brad Smith is at far right; Secretary of the Army Frank Pace is the civilian behind Truman.

reluctantly gave the order to withdraw. At this point, the task force had sustained thirty to forty casualties—far fewer than the number they would lose during the next few hours. Cohesion was soon lost. Singly or in small groups, men took to the paddy fields or tried to follow the line of the nearby railroad track. As they did so, they were subjected to a constant volume of machine-gun and mortar fire.

When Smith withdrew, he headed to Lt. Col. Millard Perry's artillery position to let him know that the infantry had pulled out. Surprisingly, he found the guns still intact. With the situation untenable, Perry's men removed the sights and breech blocks from their howitzers, then mounted up and headed south. Along the way, they picked up about 100 of Smith's infantrymen as they emerged from the rice paddies to the north. Eventually, Smith was able to assemble about 250 members of his task force, many of whom had been wounded. The others had been either killed or captured, and, of the latter, about 34 later died in North Korean prison camps. The gallant men of Task Force Smith had paid a terrible price, but they would never be forgotten. In 1951, a group of Task Force Smith veterans was honored by President Truman in a White House ceremony (3–35).

Retrograde

As the North Korean offensive continued, remnants of the ROK Army were offering resistance along a wide but thinly held front. By now, more 24th Division units were arriving in Korea and taking up positions along the crucial highway that began at Seoul and

3–36 In a ten-hour engagement, 400 Chinese were killed.

The last of Dean's regiments to arrive was the 19th Infantry, known as the Rock of Chicka-mauga. It had a special place in Dean's heart; years earlier, as a young captain, he had served with the "Chicks" in Hawaii. Dean told the men to set up and dig in along the Kum River. They might not be able to hold indefinitely, but, at least, they could buy some time for others to arrive. Engineers blew the Kum River bridges, and weary Americans waited for the attack that would come. Once again, the Americans were unable to hold. Although Chinese casualties were high (3–36), enemy troops crossed the river using barges on either flank and were soon in the rear. They set up roadblocks and hit the Americans' supporting artillery. With the enemy threatening to cut them off, the Americans were forced to retreat.

Throughout this early period, the North Korean attackers were not only successful but also remarkably consistent. The Americans would move south along main roads, find good positions, and deploy. When the North Koreans came onto an American position, they took it under fire with part of their force and, with the remainder, maneuvered to one or both flanks and took up blocking positions in the rear. At this point, they attacked. As the Americans tried to withdraw, the North Koreans inflicted heavy casualties from their blocking positions. Sometimes, the green Americans stood and fought; at

ran south to Pyongtaek, Chochi-won, Taejon, and Taegu and ended up at Pusan. The 24th Division's 34th Infantry tried in vain to stop the NKPA advance, first at Pyong-taek on July 5 and 6, and then at Chonan on July 7 and 8.

Meanwhile, the division's 21st Infantry Regiment was under attack at Chonui and taking heavy losses. At one point, it even gained some lost ground in a counterattack, and the Americans discovered, for the first time, a communist atrocity—something

that would become all too familiar in the days ahead—six American GIs, their hands tied behind their backs with barbed wire, with bullets in their heads. At another site, near Yongsan, civilian bodies were found in a ditch. On July 11, after falling back from Chonui, the 21st Infantry took up a blocking position at Chochiwon but was again driven back with heavy losses. The Gimlets were now down to about 1,100 men, fewer than half the number that had arrived from Japan.

other times, they panicked and fled in disorder. The unlovely word *bugout* became part of the GI vocabulary.

Meanwhile, the U.S. Navy and Air Force were continuing to punish the enemy, both at North Korean installations and in the battle area itself. Air attacks on NKPA armor, transport, and infantry had become so effective that the enemy no longer placed its tanks, trucks, and long columns of marching men on the roads in broad daylight (3–37 to 3–43). Tragically, however, friendly air strikes sometimes went awry and resulted in casualties among either the Americans or their South Korean allies.

There was now a new level of command in Korea. Two more American divisions, the 25th Infantry and the 1st Cavalry

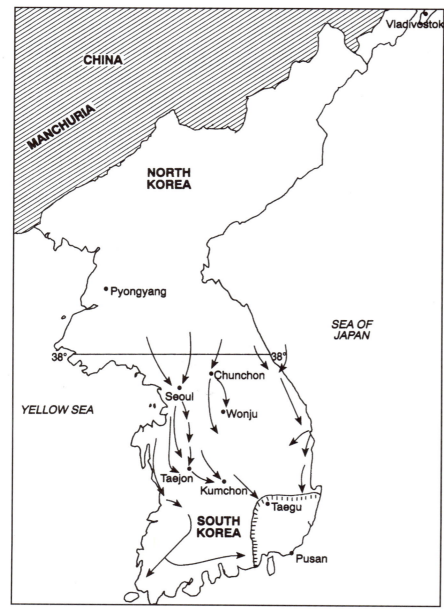

Map 3 The Invasion of South Korea

3–37 Damage done to a North Korean oil refinery in Wonsan by planes of the Seventh Fleet. Smoke could be seen 60 miles at sea.

3–38 Wreckage of a rail center at Kusong in North Korea.

3–39 Carrier planes blast North Korean bridges at Pyongyang, July 3–4, 1950.

3–40 Eight-inch turret battery of the USS *Toledo* blasts a military target in Korea.

3–42 U.S. Navy planes left factories, 5 miles north of Kwanju, engulfed in flames.

3–41 U.S. Navy planes left factories, 5 miles north of Kwanju, engulfed in flames.

3–43 Lt. Gen. Walton H. Walker (left) congratulates Maj. Dean Hess, commander of the Bout-One project, a composite unit of American and South Korean pilots flying F-51s in the early days of the war.

(also infantry, despite its name), were beginning to arrive (3–44 to 3–47), and General Walker had set up an Eighth Army headquarters. This meant that Bill Dean now had only his own 24th Division to worry about. With other units not yet engaged, however, Dean's 24th, along with the ROK allies, were the ones bearing the brunt of the fighting and taking the losses (3–47).

Although Dean's main headquarters was now back at Yong-dong, he and an advance party stayed well forward at the 34th Infantry Command Post in Taejon, a spot where he might be able to influence the action. On the morning of July 20, enemy tanks and troops fought their way into the streets of Taejon (3–48). Dean himself became caught up in the action and, at one point, was

3–44 Troops of the 13th Signal Company,
1st Cavalry Division, await letters from home.

3–45 24th Infantry Regiment of the 25th Infantry
Division prepares to move out.

3–46 Members of the 25th Infantry Division at
Pusan are bound for battle.

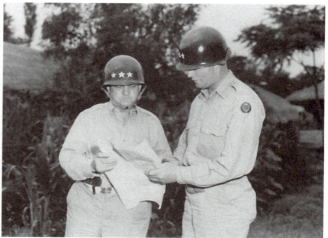

3–47 Eighth Army Commander Walton H. Walker
(left) and 24th Division Commander William F.
Dean examining a map of the front lines.

3–48 Soviet-made tanks knocked out at Taejon.

responsible for knocking out an enemy tank with a 3.5-inch rocket launcher (3–49). (By this time, as shown in photograph 3–50, a supply of 3.5s had been rushed from the States to replace the ineffective 2.36-inch bazookas.) Later that day, as the Americans were driven out of Taejon in disorder, Dean became separated from his men. After spending thirty-six days in trying to get back to friendly lines, he was led into an ambush and captured. Dean would spend the next three years as a North Korean prisoner.

As July drew to a close, ROK Army units were in the east, in the mountains, and along the coast. Those closest to the sea were being supported by naval surface forces and Navy and Marine air. Between July 20 and 30, the ROK 3d Division, in desperate fighting, made one of the few successful holding actions that had been achieved up to that time. Slowly, however, the ROK Army was being pushed back (3–51 and 3–52).

The enemy, having overcome the Americans on the main axis of advance, now headed for Korea's southwestern corner. As the NKPA 6th Division drove down the west coast, it tried to eliminate potential opposition by murdering South Korean civil servants. Having outflanked the U.S. Eighth Army, the North Koreans began an assault on Chinju. In effect, they were positioning themselves to drive on Pusan and cut off all UN forces in Korea. Moving to block them were the 19th Infantry Chicks and two battalions of the 29th Infantry Regiment, newly arrived from Okinawa.

Seven hundred men of the 29th Infantry reached their objective, the Hadong Pass, near Chinju, on July 26. There, they ran into an ambush and were soon overwhelmed. They had expected to oppose five hundred

3–49 Soviet-built T-34 tank destroyed at Taejon with an inscription crediting Maj. Gen. William F. Dean.

3–50 Three students receive instructions from an officer on the 3.5-inch bazooka.

enemy troops but found themselves outnumbered many times over. It became a massacre. Some fought their way out of the ambush, but they left three hundred to four hundred dead behind. It was a bitter introduction to combat for green American troops who had arrived in combat only the day before.

There were threats at all points, and nowhere did the enemy seem to be losing momentum. The ROK Army was falling back on the eastern flank; in the central sector, the enemy was heading for Taegu; and, in the southwest, Chinju had fallen and a battle was raging in the vicinity of Masan. If Masan were to fall, the enemy would have a clear route to Pusan.

The situation was grim, and no one knew that better than General Walker. Americans were fighting for their lives, with the distinct possibility that they, as well as their South Korean allies, would be pushed into the sea. New forces, however, were beginning to arrive. On July 31, the 9th Regiment of the U.S. 2d Infantry Division began to land at Pusan. Three days later, the 1st Marine Provisional Brigade arrived from Camp Pendleton, California; it was temporarily attached to the U.S. 25th Division and moved up to join the fighting for Masan (3–53).

With these troops now on hand in the southeastern corner of Korea, Walker believed that, by using the Naktong River as a barrier, he finally had a defensible line. Nevertheless, there could be

3–51 South Korean soldier aids a wounded buddy before he is evacuated.

3–52 South Korean soldiers in a Korean hospital at Miryang. When U.S. soldiers discovered that the South Koreans did not have cigarettes or candy, they provided these amenities to their wounded comrades from their own supplies.

no more falling back; the UN forces had run out of real estate, and further retreat would lead to disaster. Walker proceeded to issue his famous "stand or die" order. He said, in part; "A retreat to Pusan would be one of the greatest bloodbaths in American history. We must fight until the end. . . . If some of us must die, we will die fighting together. Any man who gives ground may be personally responsible for the death of thousands of his comrades. . . . I want everybody to understand that we are going to hold this line. We are going to win." (3–54)

They were brave, gallant words, even though "stand or die" had little sales appeal for those Americans rushing forward to join the team.

3–53 Aerial view of the city of Masan.

3–54 General Walker (second from right) discussing future operations with key officers.

⊣FOUR⊢
The Pusan Perimeter

The Pusan Perimeter, a thin line of weary South Koreans and Americans, was established during the first week of August 1950. Using the Naktong River (4–1) as a barrier, it extended about 100 miles north to south, about 50 miles east to west, and was anchored on the port city of Pusan. The North Koreans, hoping for an early breakthrough, were soon attacking at several points.

Not only was the situation grim for those manning the front lines, it was equally tense for their families back home, most of whom had read about Walton Walker's "stand or die" order. That order had been given extensive publicity, as had the stories of earlier defeats. Tales of American heroics could not gloss over the simple fact that the UN forces were being beaten—and badly. With television still in its infancy, this would be the last war to be covered almost exclusively by print journalists—newspaper, magazine, and wire service reporters from the Associated Press, United Press, and International News Service. When the war began, there were only five wire service correspondents in Seoul. By the time that Task Force Smith went into action on July 5, some 70 reporters were in the country. This total increased to 270 during the course of the war, a large number to be sure, but nothing to compare with Vietnam, where there would be well over 400 accredited correspondents (4–2 to 4–4).

On the newspaper maps, the Pusan Perimeter looked like a continuous line. In actuality, it was mostly a series of thinly held outposts. U.S. Army doctrine at

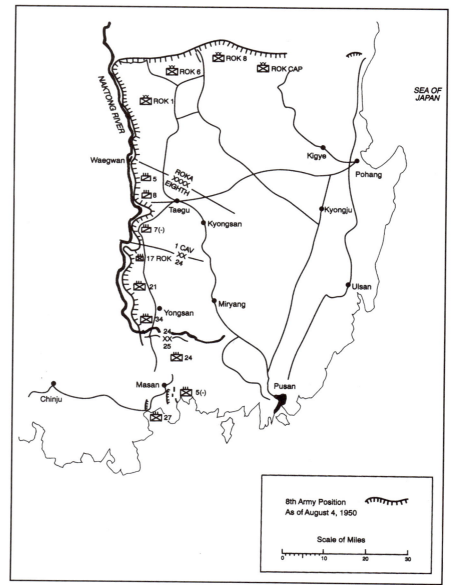

Map 4 The Pusan Perimeter as of August 4, 1950

4–1 A Marine patrol moves along the Naktong River.

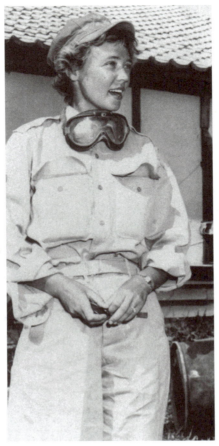

4–2 Marguerite Higgins, combat correspondent for the *New York Herald-Tribune*.

the time indicated that the practical front for a division was about 10,000 yards. In Walker's Eighth Army sector, infantry battalions, technically one ninth of a division, were often responsible for fronts of 15,000 yards or more.

By early August, nevertheless, the arrival of new units, such as the Marine Brigade, allowed the Eighth Army to begin mounting a few limited offensives (4–5 to 4–7). Along the southern coast, in the Masan sector, Task Force Kean, named for 25th Division Commander Maj. Gen. William B. Kean (4–8), attacked with elements of the 25th Division, the 1st Provisional Marine Brigade, and the 5th Regimental Combat Team (RCT), the latter newly

4–3 Combat reporter Hal Boyle of the Associated Press (center) interviews officers of the 2d Infantry Division.

4–4 Cpl. John Romanowski of Chicago was a typical army cameraman covering the war in Korea.

arrived from Hawaii (4–9). The force advanced west toward Chinju along two roads but, after some good initial progress, ran into heavy opposition. Several thousand enemy soldiers, who had infiltrated the hills between the roads, attacked in force and drove a wedge between Kean's two forces. The columns were brought to a halt, and the situation became jumbled. Fierce fighting developed, and losses were heavy on both sides (4–10 to 4–17). Particularly hard hit were the roadbound artillery units. The 555th Field Artillery Battalion (known as the "Triple Nickel") lost six of its guns, the 90th Field Artillery Battalion lost five, and about three hundred artillerymen from the two outfits were killed, wounded, or captured. (Later, the Americans learned that the NKPA had murdered twenty captured men of the 90th Field.) After five days of heavy action, Task Force Kean withdrew.

4–5 Marines waiting to embark in San Diego.

4–6 Supplies for the Marines—hundreds of tons of equipment ready for loading on board a cargo ship.

4–7 Marines march into a railway station at Pusan after disembarking from transports.

4–8 Col. Godwin Ordway (left) and Maj. Elmer G. Owens explain the local situation to Maj. Gen. William B. Kean (center), commanding general of the 25th Infantry Division.

Although Kean had failed to capture Chinju, his operation had produced some significant results. Enemy commanders were racing against time—hoping to capture Pusan and deliver a knockout blow before UN forces became too strong. The task force, by inflicting an estimated three thousand casualties on North Korea's 6th Division, had stopped the southern prong of the offensive and severely interfered with the communist timetable.

Throughout this period, America's control of the skies became doubly significant. Marine units, lacking the army's heavy artillery, had traditionally concentrated on developing a close air support capability. Beginning with the Task Force Kean operation, marine aircraft were flying close support missions and marine helicopters were on hand to perform medical evacuations (4–18). Close support of ground troops, on the other hand, had not been a priority for the U. S. Air Force. Now, however, the U. S. Fifth Air Force of Maj. Gen. Earle E. Partridge (4–19) had to provide not only close air support to front line units but also maintain a comprehensive interdiction campaign, the latter concentrating on destroying road and rail bridges on routes leading to the battle area. Propeller-driven aircraft, F-51 Mustangs (4–20 and 4–21) or Marine or Navy F-4U Corsairs (4–22 and 4–23) flew most of the close support missions. For interdiction or hitting strategic targets in North Korea, fighter-bombers, B-26 light bombers (4–24 to

4–9 Men of the 5th RCT hunt for snipers in a burned-out village.

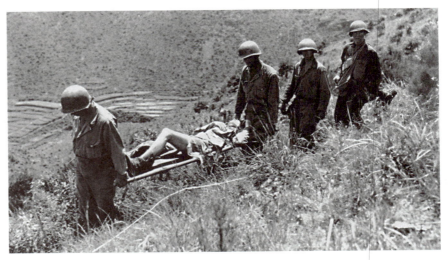

4–10 Medics carry wounded soldiers of the 5th RCT in the Masan area.

4–11 North Koreans lie dead beside a house. They were killed in an attempt to retreat near Taegu.

4–13 A grief-stricken American infantryman, whose buddy has been killed in action near Haktong-Ni, is comforted by another soldier. In the background, a corporal fills out casualty tags.

4–12 A bullet-pierced helmet and a dead soldier on the way to Masan.

4–14 A wounded man of the 7th Marines is taken to the rear.

4–15 Graveyard of enemy tanks: three T-33s destroyed on Hill 125. In the foreground are the bodies of three Marines.

4–16 After their first big battle, weary Marines rest.

4–17 Marines take cover from mortar fire.

4–18 A USMC pilot warms up a helicopter in preparation for evacuating the wounded.

4–26), and B-29 Superfortresses (4–27 to 4–29) were the work-horses.

To improve matters further, U.S. medium tanks, now on the scene, were able to compete with the enemy's T-34. Earlier, the lone American tank to see action had been the light M-24 General Chaffee, which mounted an ineffectual 75-mm gun. In Japan, each of the four infantry divisions had been authorized a heavy tank battalion; however, only one company in each battalion had been organized and equipped with the light M-24s, rather than heavy tanks (4–30). The first tankers to arrive were the armor school troops from Fort Knox, men of the 70th Tank Battalion equipped with M-26 Pershings mounting 90-mm guns and M-4A3E8 Shermans (76-mm guns) (4–31 and 4–32). The battalion was so short of tanks that those on concrete pedestals as monuments around Fort Knox had to be taken down and made operational by

4–19 Lt. Gen. Earle E. Partridge (center), Commander, Far East Air Forces, talks with USAF Chief of Staff Hoyt Vandenberg (left) and other officers.

4–20 Unusual photo of an F-51 Mustang releasing two napalm bombs. A sister plane at the far left will assist.

4–21 A Mustang taxis through a miniature lake formed by torrential Korean rains.

4–22 Planes of Task Force 77—bomb-laden Corsairs ready for deck launch—await the signal to taxi into position.

4–23 F-4U Corsair, with an extra gas tank, in flight.

4–24 B-26 light bombers release 500-pound bombs in a strike over North Korea.

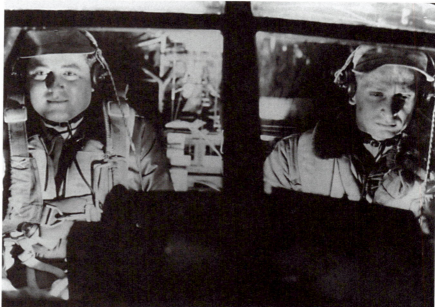

4–25 The navigator and the pilot of a 5th Air Force B-26 are ready for a night intruder mission over enemy territory. An aerial gunner rounds out the crew.

4–26 Bombardiers in B-26s use the "Y" in the track as an aiming point with uncanny accuracy.

4–27 B-29s dropping bombs on targets in the north inflicted heavy damage on cities and industries.

installing engines, transmissions, and other equipment. Ammunition shortage was also a problem, as was the amount of ammunition that had deteriorated in storage. The United States not only had failed to replenish its supplies after World War II but the entire ammunition industry had been dismantled. Understandably, postwar America had shifted its focus; its main interest was producing goods for a booming consumer economy.

Meanwhile, still other armor units were being rushed to Korea. The Marine Brigade came with its own M-26 Pershings (4–33). The Infantry School's 73d Tank Battalion, also with M-26s, after initially being under Eighth Army was later attached to the 7th Infantry Division. The 6th Tank Battalion, equipped with brand-new M-46 Pattons (90-mm guns), was eventually attached to the 24th Infantry Division (4–34).

On August 8, a penetration by the NKPA 4th Division resulted in what became known as the First Battle of the Naktong Bulge. Everyone was thrown into the fight. Even squads of combat engineers, men who normally would be building bridges, found themselves manning frontline foxholes. After ten days of heavy fighting, the 24th Infantry Division, reinforced by the 1st Marine Provisional Brigade brought up from Task Force Kean, and ele-

4–28 B-29s strike a North Korean bridge with deadly accuracy from 10,000 feet.

4–29 B-29s striking railroad bridges.

4–30 An M-24 tank did not quite make it through this narrow pass on a road north of Sungan-ni. Note the dead crewmen hanging from the tank hatch.

4–31 M-26 Pershing tanks are test fired at Taegu.

4–32 Advancing ROK infantrymen scout a road accompanied by American M-4 tanks.

4–33 Marines of a Pershing tank crew eat chow somewhere in Korea.

4–34 Tanks of the 6th Tank Battalion, 24th Infantry Division, lay down support fire for men of the 19th Infantry Regiment.

ments of the U.S. 2d and 25th Infantry Divisions, were able to contain and reduce the salient. By August 19, the NKPA 4th Division had been nearly destroyed as a fighting force. Although the Americans had also paid a heavy price (4–35 to 4–38), the river line had been restored.

Elsewhere along the perimeter, some of the heaviest fighting involved the 1st Cavalry Division, whose commander, Maj. Gen. Hobart R. ("Hap") Gay (4–39), was responsible for a front 35

4–35 Wounded American soldiers receiving treatment.

4–36 Soldiers receiving blood plasma while being loaded on an L-5 light airplane.

4–37 A man replaces headboards with crosses on graves of the 1st Cavalry Division near Taegu.

4–38 Funeral services for Howell G. Thomas, the District of Columbia's first Korean War casualty to be interred at Arlington National Cemetery.

miles long. All the fifty-six-year-old Gay could do was to outpost likely avenues of approach and hope to eject the enemy by counterattacks. Helping Gay initially by manning the Cavalry's southern flank was the 1st Battalion, 23d Infantry Regiment, of Maj. Gen. Lawrence ("Dutch") Keiser's 2d Division. On September 5, this battalion was returned to its parent division, and the newly arrived 27th British Commonwealth Brigade took its place on line. The British, arriving from Hong Kong and led by Brig. Basil A. Coad, had two battalions, one from the Middlesex Regiment, and the other from the Argyll and Sutherland Highlanders (4–40 and 4–41). The British arrival was a solid morale boost for both ROK and American troops. Back in the States meanwhile, other UN members were pledging their support. It was feared, however, that weeks or even months might elapse before other UN elements were

4–39 Maj. Gen. Hobart R. Gay, Commander, 1st Cavalry Division (left), and Lt. Col. William Harris, 77th Field Artillery, observe the effectiveness of fire.

4–40 British sergeant oversees the disembarking of his men from the H.M.S. *Ceylon* at Pusan.

4–41 Motor platoon, 1st Battalion, Argyll and Sutherland Highlanders, prepares to move to the front at the Naktong River west of Taegu.

4–42 Artillery shells burst on Hill 303, north of Waegwan.

physically present. By then their help might be too late.

The 5th Cavalry Regiment was deployed north of the British to defend a sector that included the Naktong around Waegwan, including the infamous Hill 303 (4–42) and the main road running southeast from there to Taegu. On August 15, American prisoners captured on Hill 303 were executed in cold blood; 1st Cavalry troopers later named the place "Atrocity Hill." One of those killed on Hill 303 was 2d Lt. Cecil Newman (4–43), who had graduated from West Point in June 1949 and, before attending West Point, had seen infantry combat in World War II.

The 7th Cavalry Regiment, in line next to the 5th, was the famed Garry Owen Regiment, whose history traced back to the days of George Armstrong Custer

4–43 2d Lt. Cecil Newman, murdered on Hill 303 by North Korean troops, along with 302 other American prisoners.

4–44 South Korean soldier operating a flamethrower.

4–45 A sniper's view of the wreckage at Pohang.

and the Battle of the Little Big Horn. Next, on the 1st Cavalry Division's right flank, the 8th Cavalry Regiment fought in the mountains on either side of the Sangju road. It was a seesaw battle, with hills being taken, retaken, and then taken again. Meanwhile, on the east coast, the port city of Pohang was captured by the North Koreans and then retaken by the ROK Army after a fierce counterattack (4–44 to 4–46).

More heavy fighting was taking place west of Taegu along a critical highway that became known as the "Bowling Alley." Over a six-day period, August 15–20, the 27th Infantry Regiment Wolfhounds of the U.S. 25th Infantry Division,

holding on gamely, repelled a series of attacks that resulted in heavy enemy losses in both troops and equipment.

As reinforcements continued to arrive, they were being supported by new logistical organizations—the Pusan Base Depot, organized on August 12, and the

Japan Logistical Command, set up on August 25 to provide supplies to the war in Korea and to assume the occupation duties of the Eighth Army (4–47 and 4–48). For the Eighth Army itself, new sources of manpower, with the concurrence of Syngman Rhee, were the recruits known as

KATUSAs (Korean Augmentations to the U.S. Army). Each company-sized unit was authorized one hundred men, technically part of the ROK Army but fed, trained, and equipped by the Americans. Some companies set up a buddy system pairing one KATUSA with one American; other put the new recruits into separate Korean platoons. Despite the obvious problems with language, the experiment paid off. Frontline units were more than happy to have added manpower shoring up the porous perimeter (4–49 to 4–51).

4–46 Ruins of Pohangdong. Note that the center of the city is completely burned out.

4–47 Port facilities stockpiled with military supplies along the docks in Pusan.

4–48 An American soldier supervises the storing of cartons of C rations in Pusan.

4–49 Coauthor Harry Maihafer, then executive officer of I Company, 21st Infantry Regiment, with one of his unit's KATUSA soldiers.

In addition to the KATUSAs, many other Koreans were pressed into service, performing much needed manual labor. This included the familiar "chiggi bearers," strong, wiry men who used A-frames to carry rations and ammunition to frontline troops (4–52 to 4–54). Also, as the pitiful refugee stream kept flowing south, many homeless orphans left the column to be "adopted" as mascots by compassionate Americans. Dressed in cut-down GI uniforms, these youngsters became unofficial members of American combat units as they lived alongside and traveled with their newfound GI friends (4–55).

When the perimeter had been established in early August, the ROK Army was down to five decimated divisions and it desperately needed to activate new units. Training centers and schools were set up to help in building new divisions and providing a flow of replacements for existing divisions. At first, KMAG plans called for a ten-day recruit training cycle that emphasized rifle marksmanship. Unfortunately, even this short period had to be reduced because of the critical need for replacements at the front. Recruit training was hampered further by the lack of weapons and equipment. Early in the war, the ROK Army's most critical losses had been among its officers and non-commissioned officers (NCOs). Special courses were set up to replenish these ranks, including a two-week NCO school and a six-week officer candidate school, the latter having four weeks of general training and two weeks of specialized branch training (4–56 and 4–57). By this time, the North Korean ranks had been depleted, not only because of those killed, wounded, or captured but also from the effects of malnutrition

4–50 Pvt. Yun Chun, age fifteen, a KATUSA assigned to the 19th Infantry Regiment, 24th Division. According to his American officers, he was one of the best. He allegedly held a hill overnight with his M-1 rifle.

4–51 Cpl. Richard Tablante of San Francisco, and Cpl. Erland D. Oregne of Soldier's Grove, Wisconsin, members of Company C, 1st Battalion, 9th Regiment, 2d Infantry Division, lead five ROK soldiers on a patrol near Tohosan.

4–52 South Korean civilians help to carry captured weapons.

4–53 South Korean workmen carry rocks for the foundation of an earth bridge for the 1st Cavalry Division.

4–54 South Koreans, who are too old to fight, help to build an airstrip.

4–56 ROK Noncommissioned Officer's School.

4–55 "Little Joe," a South Korean orphan adopted by a medical company of the 25th Infantry Division proudly displays a North Korean weapon to Sgt. Clarence Hallis of Akron, Ohio.

4–57 ROK troops attend a class on mortar tactics at a training center in Korea.

4–58 Marines bring in prisoners.

4–59 North Korean captives taken on the west bank of the Naktong River by soldiers of the 5th Regimental Combat Team, 24th Infantry Division.

and disease (4–58 to 4–61). Although UN commanders were slow to realize it, their troops now outnumbered the enemy's. By early August, 141,000 troops were inside the perimeter, although only 92,000 were combat arms. The North Koreans were down to about 70,000 troops, but they managed to keep up the pressure. For psychological reasons, Kim Il Sung had ordered his commanders to take Pusan by August 15, the anniversary of the Japanese surrender. With the North Koreans mounting successive attacks and almost ignoring their staggering losses, their further penetration resulted in what became the Second Battle of the Naktong Bulge. This, too, was beaten back.

From the first days of the war, beginning with Task Force Smith, the Americans had been rushed into battle with patchwork units. The mission was to stop the enemy; if unit integrity had to suffer, so be it. The 24th Division, for example, did not fight as a unit until the First Battle of the Naktong Bulge, a full month after arriving in Korea. The two battalions of the 29th Infantry from Okinawa were each thrown into separate battles as soon as they arrived, and each suffered badly. The 5th RCT was first attached to the 25th Division, then later to the 24th Division. When it arrived in Korea, the 9th Infantry Regiment of the 2d Division was immediately attached to the 24th Division during the First Battle of the Naktong Bulge. Even after the perimeter was formed, units were constantly shifted from place to place and from one parent unit to another. The 27th Infantry Wolfhounds were typical; they detached from the 25th Division and operated independently during almost the entire month of August. Despite the organizational confusion, however, the job was getting done, and no one worried about neat organization charts or bureaucratic order of battle. The concentration was on survival. Unfortunately not everyone did. The 34th Infantry Regiment, for example, had suffered so heavily that it was disbanded at the end of August and its remaining members transferred to the other 24th Division regiments, the 19th and 21st. Normally, breaking up a unit would have caused a severe problem with unit loyalty. In this case, however, there were not enough people left to be disturbed; of the 2,000 men who had come from Japan, only 184 remained. The others had been killed or wounded or were missing.

By mid-September, the tide had turned. Not only had the UN forces strengthened but the enemy had made some serious mistakes. Instead of concentrating on one all-out thrust toward Pusan, it had dissipated its forces in a series of separate offensives, each of which had been beaten back. The North Koreans had gone as far as they were going to go. The Pusan Perimeter had held.

4–60 Wounded North Koreans eat in a hospital tent.

4–61 American soldiers of the 25th Infantry Division proudly display a captured North Korean flag.

FIVE

Inchon

On September 15, 1950, the Korean War took a dramatic new turn as American forces stormed ashore at Inchon. A classic operation, it was one of the most memorable in American military history. Also, it might have been Douglas MacArthur's finest hour.

From the early days of the war, MacArthur had contemplated an amphibious landing behind enemy lines. His "grand plan" was first to isolate the battlefield by the use of air power to seal off supply routes at the Chinese and Soviet borders. After the battlefield had been isolated and stabilized, he would land at Inchon and cut off enemy forces to the south. The Eighth Army would then advance north and close the pincers. In the summer of 1950, however, there simply were not enough troops to attempt such an operation. By that time, in fact, UN forces were doing all they could just to survive.

A high-level meeting was held at MacArthur's headquarters in the Dai Ichi Building on July 13, 1950. On hand from Washington were Army Chief of Staff J. Lawton Collins and Air Force Chief of Staff Hoyt S. Vandenberg (5–1). Other officers present included MacArthur's Chief of Staff Edward M. ("Ned") Almond (5–2). Eighth

5–1 Gen. Hoyt S. Vandenberg, U.S. Air Force Chief of Staff, at Haneda Air Force Base, Tokyo, Japan.

5–2 Maj. Gen. Edward M. ("Ned") Almond, General MacArthur's chief of staff.

Army Commander Lt. Gen. Walton H. Walker, and the Commander in Chief, Pacific Fleet, Adm. Arthur W. Radford.

Arguing for the Inchon plan, MacArthur said that he was facing a determined, aggressive enemy. Although he did not believe that the Soviet Union wanted an all-out war, he thought that the Soviets would provide maximum covert support to the North Koreans through China and Manchuria. Therefore, MacArthur said, the United States should make a maximum effort without "delay or halfway measures." And a decisive communist defeat in

Korea, he said, would check the spread of communism elsewhere in the world.

Collins and Vandenberg were not so sure, either about Inchon or about an all-out effort. A major troop commitment to the Far East would leave Europe dangerously weakened. What if the Korean attack were only a feint, a way to distract America from a major Soviet thrust into Germany? As in World War II, American leaders were far more concerned with Europe than with the Far East. In short, the Joint Chiefs were definitely lukewarm about the risky Inchon proposal.

The Joint Chiefs were right—Inchon *was* risky, incredibly so. For one thing, its tidal range, exceeding 30 feet, was one of the highest in the world. Numerous islands covered the seaward approaches; if the largest of these, Wolmi-do, were to be fortified, any craft trying to pass could be blasted out of the water. To complicate the problem, the channel was narrow and treacherous, and, with that much water flowing in, the current was 5 to 6 knots.

As the senior officials considered MacArthur's Inchon proposal (5–3), they knew that any amphibious landing was hazardous, even one without Inchon's peculiar problems. Understandably, opposition came from all sides. Chairman of the Joint Chiefs Omar Bradley thought that the day of a major amphibious operation had passed. Army Chief of Staff Collins, while liking the concept, thought that Inchon was too far in the enemy's rear; a linkup with the Eighth Army would take so long that the invasion force might be left high and dry. Moreover, even if the landing forces were successful, they would still have to cross the broad Han River before reaching their main objective of Seoul. Collins suggested a more modest alternative, perhaps a port such as Kunsan, 100 miles farther south.

For a host of technical and logistical reasons, the Navy was also opposed to the operation. One admiral said, "We drew up a list of every natural and geographic handicap to a landing

5–3 Senior U.S. officials gather to discuss the Inchon landing proposal. Guests included Secretary of State Dean Acheson, members of the Joint Chiefs of Staff, and the Secretaries of Defense, the Army, Navy, and Air Force.

and *Inchon had them all.*" MacArthur, however, was adamant. During World War II, he and the U.S. Navy had often failed to see eye to eye, but he said, "The Navy has never turned me down yet." Somewhat reluc-

5–4 Rear Adm. James H. Doyle, Commander, Naval Assault Force, at Inchon.

tantly, the Joint Chiefs approved the plan. On July 23, Chief of Naval Operations Adm. Forrest P. Sherman arrived in Tokyo to work out the details. Accompanying him were General Collins and Rear Adm. James H. Doyle (5–4), who would command the Naval Assault Force.

Planners began putting together an invasion force, but it was not easy. Throughout the summer, it had been necessary to give priority of men and materiel to frontline troops on the embattled Pusan Perimeter. Finally, however, a new X Corps came into being. Many Navy and Marine officers believed the landing, primarily a Marine show, should be controlled by Marine Lt. Gen. Lemuel C. Shepherd, Jr. (5–5), who commanded Fleet Marine Forces, Pacific, directly under Pacific Fleet Commander Radford. Nevertheless, MacArthur selected Army

5–5 Gen. Lemuel C. Shepherd, Jr. (center), Commander, 5th Marine Forces Pacific, during the Korean War, shown later as commandant.

5–6 General Almond (left) and Lieutenant General Shepherd go ashore in the launch of the USS *Mt. McKinley*.

5–7 Maj. Gen. Oliver P. Smith and Rear Adm. James H. Doyle confer on board the USS *Rochester*.

5–8 Maj. Gen. David G. Barr, Commander, 7th Infantry Division.

Maj. Gen. Ned Almond for the job (5–6). At least temporarily, Almond would remain as MacArthur's chief of staff while he also served as X Corps commander. It was an unusual arrangement, to say the least, and it was particularly resented by those who disliked the imperious Almond. It was decided that X Corps' main units would be the 1st Marine Division of fifty-seven-year-old Maj. Gen. Oliver P. Smith (5–7) and the 7th Infantry Division, led by fifty-five-year-old Maj. Gen. David G. Barr (5–8). When the 7th Division was ordered to join the invasion force, its strength was 8,800, rather than the authorized 18,000. From the first days of the war, soldiers had been taken from the 7th Division to bolster the Eighth Army—about 1,300 key officers and men had gone to beef up the 24th and 25th Divisions. Almost as a desperation measure, hastily drafted Korean civilians helped to bring the 7th Division up to strength. Assembling a full Marine division also required some fast shuffling; it meant not only using the Marine Brigade then fighting in the perimeter but also transferring people from the Mediterranean via Suez. At almost the last minute, and barely in time, the brigade was withdrawn from the perimeter so as to mount up for the invasion. Two ROK units, an ROK Marine regiment, and the 17th ROK Infantry Regiment were also added to the invasion force (5–9 and 5–10). They were welcome reinforcements, and it also made sense, politically and psychologically, for ROK units to help liberate Seoul.

Of all the services, the U.S. Navy was best equipped to handle the Inchon mission. It set up Joint Task Force 7 with Vice Adm. Arthur D. Struble (5–11)

5–9 ROK Army embarking for the Inchon invasion.

5–10 ROK soldiers being briefed by a regimental commander.

5–11 Vice Adm. Arthur D. Struble, Commander, Joint Task Force 7.

5–12 Landing beaches on Wolmi-do.

5–13 Combat-loaded Marine aircraft.

5–14 S/Sgt. Carl W. Peters (left) and Sgt. Melvin R. Bataway (right) prepare aircraft ordnance on the flight deck of the USS *Sicily*.

5–15 U.S. Marines load their equipment and supplies at Kobe, Japan, in preparation for the Inchon operation.

in command. It also provided air cover, shore bombardment, blockade, minesweeping, and logistics support for Admiral Doyle's attack force. Altogether, about 260 vessels were involved, creating a substantial armada.

The bombardment of Wolmi-do began on September 10 (5–12). For the next two days, Marine aircraft scorched the hump-backed island with napalm (5–13 and 5–14). On September 13, the U.S. cruisers *Toledo* and *Rochester*

arrived and began blasting away with their 8-inch main batteries. Joining the bombardment were two Royal navy cruisers, the *Kenya* and the *Jamaica*, followed by a six-ship destroyer squadron whose 5-inch guns pounded Wolmi-do unmercifully. When the destroyers left, Navy and Marine aircraft resumed the attack.

Meanwhile, the first elements of the X Corps invasion force had put to sea, the Marines embarking from Kobe and the Army from

Yokohama (5–15 to 5–18). Conditions on board the ships were crowded and uncomfortable, but the true misery lay just ahead. On the second day at sea, the convoy ran into Typhoon Kezia and its winds of 125 miles per hour. Hour after hour, violent, stormy seas tossed the ships about, with a foreseeable impact on already nervous stomachs. Men told each other that they would gladly trade the sea for the shore, even a shore defended by hostile North Koreans!

5–16 ROK Marines preparing to fight.

5–17 U.S. Marines board a troopship in Japan for their voyage to the objective.

5–18 Marines eating breakfast on the morning of D-day.

5–19 Landing ship medium rockets (LSMRs) soften up shore defenses as Marines assault Wolmi Island. Note that Wolmi is connected to Inchon by a causeway.

At 6:30 A.M. on September 15 at early high tide, the 3d Battalion of Col. Ray Murray's 5th Marines stormed ashore at Wolmi-do (5–19 and 5–20). Within forty-five minutes, the Marines had the island under control, although several more hours passed before the last North Korean defenders were pried out of their holes (5–21). Murray, a thirty-seven-year-old World War II veteran of Guadalcanal, Tarawa, and Saipan, was no stranger to amphibious landings. His regiment was one of the best; not only were his men physically tough, well trained, and well armed but they were supported by their own Marine close air support. (Army units had to request Air Force close-support missions through a slow, cumbersome process. Throughout the war, soldiers envied the efficient, on-call air support provided by the 1st Marine Aircraft Wing of Maj. Gen. Field Harris (5–22).)

Some eleven hours later, around 5 P.M. at the next high tide, the main assault force headed

5–20 Members of the 1st Marine Division head for Blue Beach on Wolmi Island.

5–21 Dead North Korean soldiers on Wolmi Island.

5–22 Maj. Gen. Field Harris, Commander, 1st Marine Aircraft Wing.

for Inchon (5–23 and 5–24). Murray's other two battalions, followed by ROK Marines, went in on the left at Red Beach; three battalions of Col. Lewis B. ("Chesty") Puller's 1st Marine Regiment aimed for Blue Beach on the right. As soon as the LCVPs (landing craft, vehicle, personnel) hit the stone sea walls, ladders and grappling hooks were thrown out and Marines scrambled up and over (5–25 and 5–26). Thanks to covering fire laid down from Wolmi-do, resistance was soon stifled on Red Beach. At Blue Beach, despite some initial confusion partly caused by smoke and haze from the naval bombardment, Puller soon had things sorted out and under control. By midnight of D-day, the Inchon landing was a definite success. Casualties had been surprisingly light, and about thirteen thousand Marines were ashore with their weapons and equipment. Douglas MacArthur, watching the operation from Doyle's flagship, the USS *Rochester*, knew that his gamble had paid off. "The Navy has never shone more brightly," MacArthur said (5–27). Twenty-four hours later, the high ground east of Inchon was secured, thus preventing enemy artillery fire from hitting the landing and unloading area (5–28 and 5–29). With Inchon secure and encircled, it

5–23 LCVPs from the USS *Union* prepare to land at Inchon.

5–24 Landing craft heading to the beach.

5–26 Col. Lewis B. ("Chesty") Puller.

5–25 Waves of Leathernecks storm ashore at Inchon.

5–28 U.S. Marines in Inchon engaged in street fighting.

5–27 Gen. Douglas MacArthur (center) conferring with (left to right) Maj. Gen. Field Harris, USMC, and Rear Adm. James H. Doyle on board the USS *Rochester*.

5–29 Men of the 1st Marine Division advancing through Inchon.

5–30 Supplies on Inchon's beaches after the invasion.

5–31 South Korean refugees return to Inchon.

5–32 North Korean tank in flames.

was unlikely that any enemy still in the city could escape. ROK Marines moved in to mop up. On the evening of September 16, Marine Maj. Gen. Oliver P. Smith established his command post east of Inchon and notified Admiral Doyle that he was assuming responsibility for operations ashore (5–30 and 5–31).

The Marines pushed on in two columns that generally followed the line of the Inchon-Seoul highway. F-4U Corsairs, taking off from the carrier *Sicily*, spotted six enemy T-34 tanks accompanied by infantry on the highway east of Seoul. The Corsairs dropped 500-pound bombs and napalm, destroyed the tanks, and scattered the infantry. On the left, Murray's 5th Marines headed for Kimpo airfield and the Han River just beyond it. On the right, Puller's 1st Marines headed toward Yongdung-po, Seoul's large industrial suburb on the south bank of the Han. In early darkness on the morning of September 17, six more T-34 tanks, accompanied by about 250 North Korean infantrymen, approached the lines of the 5th Marines. Combined fire from Pershing tanks, recoilless rifles, and 3.5-inch rocket launchers destroyed all six tanks and killed an estimated 200 infantry (5–32 and 5–33). By the next morning, Kimpo airfield was secured. That afternoon, a Marine Corsair landed at Kimpo, and, later in the day, Brig. Gen. Thomas Cushman's Marine Air Group 33 flew in from Japan (5–34 to 5–36).

5–33 North Korean POWs march past a destroyed T-34 tank.

5–34 Members of the 1st Marine Division set up a field stove near the remains of a Soviet-type Il-3 airplane at Kimpo.

5–35 U.S. Marines relax in the burned-out headquarters building at Kimpo.

5–36 F-4U Corsair from the USS *Philippine Sea* at Kimpo airfield.

Meanwhile, as Puller's 1st Marines arrived at the outskirts of Yongdung-po, other elements of Ned Almond's X Corps were coming ashore, and Almond arrived to set up his X Corps headquarters. The last of Smith's regiments, the 7th Marines, had landed on the 17th; units of Barr's 31st and 32d Infantry Regiments landed on the 18th and 19th. On the evening of September 19, the 32d Infantry assumed responsibility for the zone south of the highway. At this point, a dispute arose between the Marines and Corps Commander Almond. Somewhat arbitrarily, Almond said the Marines were moving too slowly. He wanted a wide envelopment so as to attack Seoul from the southeast and suggested that Smith give the job to Puller's 1st Marines. Smith objected, saying he didn't want to split his two regiments or have his men going into Seoul from two different directions. The furious Almond, determined to take Seoul by September 25 (three months to the day from the war's beginning), gave the job to Col. Charles

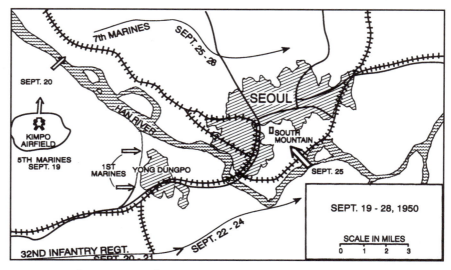

Map 5 Inchon, September 19–28, 1950

Beauchamp's 32d Infantry Regiment (5–37).

On September 25, the 32d Infantry used Marine landing craft to make an amphibious crossing of the Han and then pushed into Seoul. The ROK 17th Regiment crossed behind the 32d Regiment (5–38 to 5–40). Simultaneously, Smith's Marine regiments came in from the west. The official communiqué of September 25 stated

5–37 Col. Charles Beauchamp (left), Commander, 32d Infantry Regiment.

5–38 AMTRACs advancing across the Han River toward Seoul.

5–39 American troops on their way to retake Seoul.

5–40 M-4 tank rolling off a pontoon bridge after crossing the Han River.

5–41 Americans forcing four North Korean troops from a bunker.

5–42 Six North Korean captives being searched.

5–43 Rhee expresses his gratitude to UN forces and to General MacArthur at the liberation. Rhee (holding paper) stands behind podium. Directly facing him is General MacArthur.

5–44 South Korean citizens gather to celebrate the liberation of Seoul by UN forces.

5–45 ROK units parade triumphantly in newly-liberated Seoul.

that Seoul was liberated, although three days of dangerous mopping up remained. Fanatical North Korean defenders had to be rooted out street by street and, often, house by house (5–41 and 5–42).

By September 29, Seoul was sufficiently safe to permit its restoration as the seat of Syngman Rhee's government. MacArthur and Rhee flew into Kimpo airfield to stage an appropriate ceremony in the bomb-damaged National Assembly Hall in Government House (5–43). MacArthur declared the city liberated in God's name. Following this, in an emotional scene, he led the assembled group in the Lord's Prayer. After a tearful President Rhee expressed his "undying gratitude" to the American military, ROK units paraded triumphantly through the streets of Seoul (5–44 to 5–46).

Breakout from the Perimeter

The plan was for X Corps to act as the anvil, with Walker's Eighth Army and the ROKs moving up from the south to smash communist defenders against that anvil. The plan worked, but it was far more costly than Walker's Eighth Army would have liked (5–47). For example, they

5–46 ROK units parade triumphantly in newly-liberated Seoul.

expected that the Inchon landing would demoralize communist troops in the south, but communist officers never told their men about the landings. Also, while many of the troops facing the Eighth Army at this point were South Koreans conscripted against their will and obviously not wanting to fight, their officers and NCOs were quick to execute anyone reluctant to obey orders or who tried to desert.

5–47 24th Division casualties being evacuated from South Korea.

5–48 Pershing M-26 tanks cross the Kumho River on their way to the Naktong.

On September 16, after beating back an NKPA attack, the 2d Infantry Division launched an attack of its own against enemy troops that remained east of the Naktong. Both tanks and infantry moved forward, pushing the enemy against the river (5–48 to 5–50). Overhead, Air Force F-51s appeared to strafe the fleeing enemy and drop napalm. North of

5–49 A North Korean 57-mm gun captured by the 2d Division.

5–50 Maj. James Nobors of Talladega, Alabama, Operations Officer, 38th Infantry Regiment, 2d Division, examines captured documents.

5–51 Ninety-mm guns lay down a barrage in support of the 5th Regimental Combat Team.

5–52 Men of the 5th Regimental Combat Team pinned down on the banks of the Naktong River.

5–53 Tanks and infantry of the 1st Cavalry Division advancing north.

the 2d Division, following a thunderous B-29 bombardment and a heavy artillery barrage, the 5th RCT took the town of Waegwan after a hard fight (5–51 and 5–52). The next day, the 24th Division made an assault crossing of the Naktong and began moving north. Meanwhile, the 1st Cavalry Division, although running into heavy opposition west of Waegwan, managed to break through in several places and to scatter the demoralized enemy. As the North Koreans fled north, the pursuit went into high gear. The Air Force had a field day with its F-51s and F-80s out in force—bombing, strafing, and dropping napalm. The Americans, who only days before had been fighting to survive, now sensed that the tide had turned. As the 24th Division and a 1st Cavalry unit moved north, they passed scores of burned-out vehicles, countless hundreds of enemy bodies, and huge piles of abandoned equipment. They encountered little or no organized opposition. Entire NKPA units were throwing up their hands and being herded to POW enclosures (5–53 to 5–58). Nevertheless, thousands of North Koreans, who took to the hills, would reemerge later as guerrillas; many of them had swallowed communist propaganda that claimed Americans were shooting anyone taken prisoner.

To their horror, the advancing Americans came upon much evidence of communist brutality. Several thousand people had been shot, their bodies dumped in mass graves or left to rot in the open. Targeted were soldiers, landowners, priests, teachers,

5–54 Traffic jam caused by a long line of jeeps waiting to be ferried across the Kumho River.

5–56 Damaged North Korean caisson that had been adapted for pulling by oxen.

5–55 Deuce-and-a-halfs (2½-ton trucks) crossing a river 8 miles northwest of Taegu.

government officials, and anyone who might later form a core of resistance (5–59).

In the south, the 25th Division broke through, headed west along the coast, and then turned north toward Kunsan. The troops went by truck as much as possible, with tanks leading the way and fighter planes providing overhead cover. Farther inland, the 2d Division kept pace. ROK units on the east coast, who had been doing some of the war's heaviest fighting, finally drove the North Koreans out of Pohang. To do so, the nearly exhausted ROK soldiers had launched a series of attacks supported both by UN aircraft and by the 16-inch guns of "Big Mo," the battleship *Missouri* (5–60).

On September 26, a task force from the 7th Cavalry Regiment met up near Osan with elements of the 31st Infantry Regiment, a X Corps unit moving south from Inchon. Although much mopping-up remained to be done,

5–57 Five thousand communist prisoners cross the Han River on their way to a POW camp.

5–58 Senior Col. Lee Hak-ku, Chief of Staff, 13th Division, North Korean Army (right), who was captured by the 8th Cavalry Regiment near Taegu, is interrogated.

5–59 Mass grave and bodies of South Koreans, victims of communist atrocities.

5–60 The result of a salvo from the USS *Missouri* that displaced an enemy mortar position.

a historic linkup had been accomplished. Coincidentally, it had taken place near the exact spot where, on July 5, the Americans of Task Force Smith had first tried to stop the North Koreans.

About this time, word was received from Washington that President Truman had replaced Secretary of Defense Louis Johnson. The military was not sorry to see him go; in most minds, Johnson was responsible for cutting America's armed forces to the bone, with almost tragic results. The new secretary was the esteemed Gen. George C. Marshall, whom Truman had almost begged to return to government service (5–61).

With South Korea almost entirely under UN control, political and military leaders had to decide on the next step. Should they declare victory and halt at the 38th Parallel? Or, as a second option, should they cross the

5–61 U.S. Secretary of Defense George C. Marshall (left) with Lt. Gen. Matthew B. Ridgway.

parallel; go past Pyongyang, the North Korean capital; and halt at Korea's narrow waist, roughly a line running from Sinanju on the west coast to Wonsan or Hamhung on the east? The latter would, in effect, eliminate any future threat from Kim Il Sung and also provide a buffer zone between the UN and Chinese Manchuria. A third option was to cross the 38th Parallel and go all the way to the Yalu River. That was certainly the course recommended, almost demanded, by President Rhee who believed strongly that all Korea needed to be unified.

The threshold question, of course, was whether or not to cross the 38th Parallel. On September 25, a JCS directive, although full of caveats about Chinese or Soviet intervention, had recognized the need to destroy North Korea's military capability and authorized MacArthur to conduct ground actions north of the border. Then, on October 7, the UN General Assembly, after much wrangling, voted on a resolution calling for Korean unification, elections, democratic government, and the ultimate withdrawal of UN forces. The resolution passed by a vote of 47 to 5, although the Indian delegate pointed out that the motion exceeded the original UN mandate and authorized, in effect, an invasion of North Korea. By this time, in any case, the question was moot. Two days earlier, upon orders from Syngman Rhee, the ROK Army had crossed the 38th Parallel.

— SIX —

North to the Yalu

6–1 Cpl. George D. Smedley of Mount Vernon, Indiana, and Sgt. Thomas P. Montana of Yuma, Arizona, 1st Cavalry Division, keep watch along the 38th Parallel.

The General Assembly authorization to cross the 38th Parallel had been granted somewhat reluctantly, but nevertheless the die was cast. The ROK Army, having jumped the gun, had already entered North Korea. On October 9, the Eighth Army joined the offensive and mounted a general assault led by the 1st Cavalry Division (6–1 and 6–2).

When Walker's Eighth Army and Almond's X Corps linked up, many in Eighth Army had expected Almond to come under Walker's control so as to have unity of command (6–3 and 6–4). MacArthur, however, pulled X Corps off-line and made it his general reserve; he was already planning another amphibious assault, this time with Almond's X Corps landing at Wonsan on North Korea's east coast. Almond, a longtime MacArthur favorite, thereby maintained his independence.

The 1st Marines would travel by ship from Inchon to Wonsan. The 7th Division would go by road and rail all the way back to Pusan (causing huge, foreseeable traffic jams en route), board ship at Pusan, and travel up the east coast from there. By mid-October, however, it appeared that the amphibious landing would be superfluous; the ROK units were making good time and well might be in Wonsan before X Corps ever arrived. Moreover, reports had it that Wonsan harbor was heavily mined; a landing would be delayed, perhaps significantly, while the mines were being cleared.

Somewhat predictably, the invasion of North Korea brought ominous rumblings from China, where Premier Chou En-lai told the Indian ambassador that if the United States entered North Korea, China would be forced to intervene (6–5). The Indians passed this information to the British, who relayed it to Washington. Despite reports of Chinese armies massing in Manchuria, however, neither the Central Intelligence Agency (CIA) nor the U.S. State Department seemed to take

6–2 UN forces crossing the 38th Parallel.

6–4 Maj. Gen. Edward M. Almond, Commander, X Corps (left), with Army Chief of Staff J. Lawton Collins (right).

6–3 Gen. Douglas MacArthur (right) confers with Lt. Gen. Walton H. Walker, Commander, Eighth Army.

6–5 Chou En-lai, Premier of the Peoples Republic of China.

the threat too seriously, even when Chou said publicly that "the Chinese people will not tolerate foreign aggression [in Korea] nor will they supinely tolerate seeing their neighbors being savagely invaded by imperialists."

Earlier, in a radio broadcast, President Truman had sought to reassure the Chinese by disclaiming any U.S. desire for Asian terri-tory. Nevertheless, perhaps to ease his mind about the possibility of Chinese intervention, Truman decided to meet with MacArthur face to face.

The historic meeting was held at Wake Island on October 15, 1950 (6–6). In Truman's party were Omar Bradley representing the Joint Chiefs, Dean Rusk repre-senting the State Department

(6–7), Pacific Fleet Commander Arthur W. Radford, Secretary of the Army Frank Pace, and White House aid Averell Harriman (6–8). MacArthur was accompanied by a few staff officers and Ambassador to South Korea John J. Muccio.

During the discussion, Truman asked about the possibility of Chinese intervention. MacArthur assured the President that since "victory was won in Korea," there was "little possibility of the Chinese coming in." Even if they did,

MacArthur said, he would defeat them, primarily with overwhelming airpower. Although MacArthur had made the point about China in private discussions, he was asked to make the same point for the official record. He did so, again saying there was "little possibility" of the Chinese coming in. Later, MacArthur would be condemned for this statement, although it might be argued that it was the prime responsibility of Washington, not the field commander, to assess Chinese intentions.

The Wake Island meeting broke up in an atmosphere of cordiality, its participants unaware that Chinese Chairman Mao Tse-tung (6–9) had already made the decision to intervene. As Truman headed back to Washington and MacArthur to Tokyo,

6–6 President Harry S Truman (left), and Gen. Douglas MacArthur at a meeting on Wake Island.

6–7 Special Ambassador Dean Rusk of the State Department, later to become Secretary of State.

6–8 President Truman with key Korean War advisors. From left, Special Assistant Averell Harriman, Secretary of Defense George C. Marshall, Truman, Secretary of State Dean Acheson, Treasury Secretary John Snyder, Army Secretary Frank Pace, and General Omar Bradley, Chairman of the Joint Chiefs of Staff.

6–9 Chairman Mao Tse-tung (foreground).

6–10 Paratroopers of the 187th Airborne Regimental Combat Team, en route to Korea from Japan, gear up to board a C-119 Flying Boxcar.

6–11 Australian troops, preparing to eat, on a hillside along the front.

6–12 Officers of the Royal Australian Regiment confer with American officers for operations in the vicinity of Tongman-ni.

major elements of Lin Piao's Fourth Field Army were already crossing the Yalu River into North Korea. By October 20, four field armies, of thirty thousand men each, had crossed the Yalu. Three armies were positioned opposite Eighth Army units in western Korea, and one was positioned opposite X Corps in the east. By the end of October, two additional field armies were in Korea.

UN forces were growing, however, both in numbers and in striking power. A new division, the 9th, had been added to the ROK Army. The U.S. 187th Airborne Regimental Combat Team had arrived at Kimpo airfield from Japan and was now preparing for an airdrop north of Pyongyang (6–10). A battalion of the Royal Australian Regiment (6–11 and 6–12) had joined the British Commonwealth Brigade. The 65th Infantry Regiment from Puerto Rico, part of Maj. Gen. Robert Soule's (6–13) 3d Infantry Division, was on hand, as were Allied units from the Philippines, Turkey, and Thailand (6–14 to 6–16). By the end of October, an advance party of another British

6–13 Maj. Gen. Robert Soule, Commanding General, 3d Infantry Division, at Taegu airstrip.

6–14 ROK band greets Filipino troops on their arrival in Korea.

brigade, the 29th, would arrive in Korea (6–17), as would an advance party of a battalion from The Netherlands. For the drive into North Korea, this gave the UN about 350,000 troops, of whom 230,000 were combat arms.

Walker ordered his I Corps commander, Maj. Gen. Frank W. ("Shrimp") Milburn, to cross the border near Kaesong, then fan out to the western bulge of the penin-sula (6–18). The ROK II Corps was told to push ahead in the central mountains, and, in the east, the ROK I Corps would con-tinue north along the coast and head for Wonsan. Walker's recon-stituted IX Corps, led by Maj. Gen. John B. Coulter, would con-tinue to clean up bypassed enemy units in South Korea.

As these units crossed the 38th Parallel, they became involved in something of a race: Who would

6–15 Turkish troops at Pusan.

6–16 Thai troops disembarking as they prepare to join the fray.

6–17 Brig. Gen. George Taylor, Commander, 29th British Brigade.

be first into Wonsan? And who would have the honor of capturing Pyongyang, the North Korean capital? Despite the optimistic forecasts, the NKPA had not given up. The 7th Cavalry Regiment had to fight its way across the Yesong River, and other regiments of the 1st Cavalry Division, the 5th and the 8th, continued to encounter strong opposition. On October 12, north of Kaesong, Lt. Samuel S. Coursen (West Point 1949), a platoon leader in Company C, 5th Cavalry Regiment, was killed in a heroic action for which he was later awarded the Medal of Honor, one of 131 awarded during the war, 93 of them posthumously (6–19). Pushing on aggressively, however, the 24th Infantry Division and the 1st Cavalry Division, with the British Commonwealth Brigade attached, headed northwest toward Sinuiju.

6–18 Maj. Gen. Frank W. Milburn, Commander, I Corps.

6–19 Posthumous Medal of Honor winner Lt. Samuel S. Coursen.

6–20 ROK infantry advances north.

To their right, the ROK 1st Division moved northward, and, to its right, the ROK II Corps pushed on into the mountains (6–20). These were all units of Walker's Eighth Army, and a huge gap now existed between them and X Corps, which was well to the east.

The ROK 3d and Capital Divisions were in Wonsan by October 10. That same day, three large minesweepers had arrived off Wonsan, only to encounter a vast minefield. Two thousand to four thousand contact and magnetic mines had been planted by the NKPA under the supervision of Soviet technicians. The large minesweepers were ill equipped to work in shallow waters, so the Navy sent to Japan for smaller, wooden-hulled vessels. As always, mine clearing was time consuming and dangerous (6–21); in follow-up operations, two of the smaller minesweepers hit mines and sank (6–22). The ROK divisions, meanwhile, had kept going. After capturing both Hamhung and its port city of Hungnam,

6–21 Underwater demolition team en route to explode North Korean mines.

6–22 A South Korean mine-sweeper blows up in Wonsan harbor.

6–23 Traveling 33 miles in eleven hours, troops of the 7th ROK move to new positions near Singye.

6–24 Equipment of the 1st Marine Division, on board a ship off Wonsan.

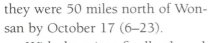
6–25 U.S. Marines landing at Wonsan.

6–26 Landing craft at Wonsan.

they were 50 miles north of Wonsan by October 17 (6–23).

With the mines finally cleared, the 1st Marines came ashore at Wonsan on October 26. For seven days, in what they sarcastically called Operation Yo-Yo, they had steamed back and forth in frustration (6–24 to 6–28). The citizens of Wonsan, who had seen Communist brutality close up, welcomed the Americans as liberators (6–29 and 6–30). The 7th Division, after waiting ten days on board ship, went farther up the coast to land at Iwon—still behind the rapidly advancing ROK Army (6–31).

To the west, Pyongyang was captured on October 19 by the ROK 1st Division and the U.S. 1st Cavalry Division (6–32 and 6–33). The following day, with MacArthur watching from the air, Brig. Gen. Frank Bowen's 187th Airborne RCT, making a parachute assault north of Pyongyang, landed at Sukchon and Sunchon and seized the two main roads leading out of the capital. Their goal was to cut off the NKPA retreat, capture government officials, and rescue American POWs. Technically, the operation was a

6–27 Captured North Koreans waiting to be shipped out from Wonsan.

6–28 Ruins at Wonsan.

6–29 A Korean woman presenting flowers to Maj. Gen. Almond.

6–30 North Koreans welcoming their liberators.

6–31 Men of the 7th Infantry Division assemble on the beaches at Iwon.

success, but, unfortunately, most of the North Korean soldiers and government officials were long gone and the POWs had been evacuated. Also, Kim Il Sung, fleeing north, had established a new capital at Sinuiju on the Yalu River opposite the Chinese city of Antung. Only one NKPA regiment, serving as a rear guard, had been trapped. The NKPA 239th, consisting of about 2,500 men, was caught between the 187th Airborne and the British Commonwealth Brigade, coming up from the south. After vicious fighting on the night of October 21–22, the paratroopers virtually annihilated the 239th Regiment—about 800 troops killed and 680 captured (6–34 to 6–39).

Tragically, as the advance continued, UN forces found more examples of communist atrocities, gruesome sites where either North

6–32 UN forces taking Pyongyang, the North Korean capital.

6–33 Mass rally by the North Korean people in their capital city of Pyongyang celebrating the occupation of the city by UN forces.

6–34 Brig. Gen. Frank Bowen (left) confers with Gen. Matthew Ridgway.

6–35 Airborne troops board a C-119 for a drop north of Pyongyang.

Korean civilians or POWs had been ruthlessly executed (6–40). At one place near a railroad tunnel, American POWs had been taken from the train in groups, supposedly to be fed. According to a weeping survivor, who had escaped by pretending to be dead, the men had been systematically killed. In one spot was a semicircle of fifteen dead Americans, many with rice bowls still in their hands, who had been shot as they waited to receive food. Altogether

6–36 Paratroopers of the 187th Airborne Regimental Combat Team readying for a jump.

6–37 Paratroopers in action.

6–38 General MacArthur peering from his airplane as he watches paratroopers drop behind enemy lines.

6–39 U.S. flag raised at Sukchon, site of the first airborne assault of the war. Four hundred troops were dropped between Sukchon and Sunchon.

there were sixty-six American corpses, not counting seven more emaciated bodies found lying on straw mats inside the tunnel. These men had either starved to death or died from disease. Many had old battle wounds (6–41).

To the east, in the X Corps sector, the ROK I Corps was moving ahead into the mountains, shortly to be followed by the U.S. 1st Marine and 7th Infantry Divisions, then by the U.S. 3d Infantry Division in reserve. Morale was high, and it seemed that victory was at hand. There was a problem, however—a serious one. Hiding in villages or hunkered down in the mountains were thousands of Chinese soldiers, still undetected and waiting to pounce.

On October 25, Chinese Communist Forces (CCF) launched their first-phase offensive when, north of Unsan, the 6th ROK Division was attacked by elements of the 50th Field Army. This attack was the first indication that China had entered the war. American intelligence officers, however, were so convinced that the war was nearly

6–41 American POWs were herded from this train and shot.

6–40 Residents of Hamhung identify the bodies of some three hundred political prisoners who suffocated in caves sealed off by North Korean soldiers.

over that they refused to believe the evidence. A few hours later, the 6th ROK Division was nearly wiped out and the ROK II Corps was in chaos.

Farther west, meanwhile, on November 1, the 21st Infantry

Gimlets of the 24th Division captured the village of Chong-go-do, 18 air miles from Sinuiju and the Yalu River. The 24th was now led by Maj. Gen. John Church, who had received his second star and taken over the division after the

capture of the unit's first commander, Bill Dean. This would turn out to be the Eighth Army's "high-water-mark." That same day, at Unsan, South Koreans and Americans were being cut off and surrounded by units of the CCF 39th Army. Before the fighting was over, the ROK 15th Infantry Regiment would be destroyed and the 8th Cavalry Regiment of Hap Gay's 1st Cavalry Division would

6–42 Cpl. Thomas A. Edwards of New York City, 8th Cavalry Regiment, is fed by Pfc. Cornelius Bosma of Ontario, California, a member of the 8063d MASH.

6–43 The first Chinese troops captured outside of Hamhung.

6–44 B-29s dropping bombs on North Korean targets.

6–45 F-80 fighter, carrying two 75-gallon tanks of napalm on its wings, heads into action.

Marines, had moved north from Iwon; one of its regiments, the 17th Infantry, reached the Yalu River near Hyesanjin. Meanwhile, between November 7 and 15, General Soule's 3d Infantry Division was disembarking at Wonsan with three fresh regiments, the 7th, the 15th, and the Puerto Rican 65th.

MacArthur hoped to seal off the northern border. On November 8, with approval from President Truman, seventy-two B-29 bombers struck Yalu River bridges at Sinuiju (6–44). On that day, the first aerial dogfight between jet aircraft occurred. Air Force Lt. Russell Brown, flying escort for the B-29s in an F-80 Shooting Star, shot down a North Korean MiG-15 jet fighter near Sinuiju (6–45).

The disappearance of the Chinese troops left everyone puzzled. By this time, intelligence officers had recognized that large numbers of CCF were in Korea. Because they seemed to be inactive, however, perhaps their appearance had been only a token effort, a Chinese effort to save face. On Thanksgiving Day, November 23, as frontline soldiers dined on roast turkey, pumpkin pie, and all the "trimmings" (6–46), wonderful rumors were circulating. There would be one quick offensive to wrap up the war, and, by Christmas, people would be heading Stateside or back to Japan.

On the day after Thanksgiving, the Eighth Army kicked off its "home by Christmas" offensive. Walker proceeded cautiously, with

lose about six hundred men (6–42). After the battle, the CCF, rather than pursuing, seemed to be disappearing into the hills.

In the X Corps sector, elements of ROK I Corps were near the Chosin Reservoir; captured Chinese prisoners had stated that large numbers of CCF were in that area (6–43). On October 30, the 1st Marine Division, having been ordered to replace the ROKs in the reservoir area, began moving from Wonsan to an assembly point near Hamhung. The 7th Infantry Division, east of the

6–46 Chaplain Burgess Riddle holds Thanksgiving Day services on the banks of the Yalu River.

6–47 Maj. Gen. Oliver P. Smith, Commander, 1st Marine Division.

his three corps in line, the U.S. I and IX on his left flank and the ROK II on his right. They would advance toward the Yalu more or less abreast so as not to leave anyone isolated. Almond's X Corps situation was different because his right-flank unit, the ROK Capital Division, was already on the border. Next to it, the U.S. 7th Division was also touching Manchuria. His main effort would be the 1st Marine Division attacking northwest toward the Chosin Reservoir area. If all went according to plan and both Eighth Army and X Corps reached their objectives, they could move toward the center— Eighth Army from the west and X Corps from the east, thereby cutting off any Chinese caught between them. But, events did not go according to plan.

On the evening of November 25, the CCF XIII Army Group launched its second-phase offen-sive on the Eighth Army front. Either by design or by chance, the CCF hit the weakest point, the 8th ROK Division of II Corps, on the inland flank. Out of the darkness, hordes of Chinese sud-denly appeared. Screaming and blowing bugles, they shattered the 8th Division and sent it flying back in disorder. Within hours, the attack had spread to the ROK 7th and 6th Divisions; they, too, were broken and overpowered by wave after wave of swarming Chi-nese. The U.S. 2d Infantry Divi-sion, on the right flank of IX Corps, suddenly found itself with an open flank. Farther west, the CCF hit the ROK 1st Division, located in the middle of I Corps. It was a good division. Although it was forced to give ground, it managed to hold, but the Eighth Army's offensive had come to an abrupt halt.

In the X Corps sector, Oliver Smith's 1st Marine Division was moving toward the Chosin Reser-voir area (6–47). Despite orders from Corps Commander Almond to move with all haste, Smith was proceeding cautiously. On November 25, X Corps issued an ambitious and highly controver-sial attack order, one which seemed to assume that the CCF units opposing X Corps were of little consequence. The Marines would concentrate west of the Chosin Reservoir, and Task Force McLean from the 7th Division (Col. Allan McLean's 31st Infantry Regiment, less one battalion, plus Lt. Col. Don Faith's 1st Battalion, 32d Infantry) would go into posi-tion east of Chosin. Both forces would launch an attack two days later, on November 27. For the 7th Division, it became a scramble even to get into position within the two days allotted. Most of its units were 100 miles away, at or near the Yalu.

On November 27, as the offensive kicked off, the Marines were concentrated at three points along an 80-mile icy road that ran to the reservoir from the port of Hungnam. Chesty Puller's 1st Marine Regiment, along with some Royal Marines and Army infantry, was at Koto-ri, about 50 miles from the coast. Smith was at Hagaru-ri, 12 miles north of Puller, where engineers were carving out an airstrip. Farthest north and west of the reservoir were the 5th and 7th Marine Regiments. East of Chosin, with Task Force McLean in the lead, were the rest of the 7th Infantry Division's 31st and 32d Regiments and the 57th Field Artillery Battalion.

In the Eighth Army sector, the CCF offensive had been in full swing by November 26, with masses of troops flowing south, setting up roadblocks, and, whenever possible, seizing the high ground. Walker tried to use Dutch Keiser's 2d Division to shore up his right flank, and reserves were committed on Keiser's right. The Turks, the 1st Cavalry Division, and the Commonwealth Brigade all went in gamely but to no avail. Walker, his line broken, and having suffered heavy losses, was forced to order a general retreat. The 2d Division, acting as the Eighth Army's rear guard, began working its way south, but a full Chinese division was waiting. Keiser's convoy was ambushed near Kunu-ri with appalling losses, some three thousand men plus all of the division vehicles. Thanks to almost continuous air support and to the British, who drove north to clear a blocked pass, about four thousand of the original seven thousand troops managed to survive.

The massive Chinese intervention had shocked the people in Washington. Army Chief of Staff Collins headed for Korea to confer with both Walker and Almond (6–48). During a press conference, Truman refused to rule out

6–48 U.S. Army Chief of Staff J. Lawton Collins (right) conferring with X Corps Commander Almond at the Hamhung airstrip.

6–49 Lined up bumper to bumper, this chain of vehicles inches along a road. Withdrawing from Hongchon to Wonju, a distance of 36 miles, took ten and one-half hours.

6–50 U.S. Marines move south from Koto-ri.

6–52 Marine base at the foot of the Chosin Reservoir.

6–51 Bitter cold, bitter fight.

the possible use of nuclear weapons. Clearly, the CCF XIII Army Group had the momentum. By December 5, the Eighth Army had abandoned Pyongyang. South of the capital, a new defensive line was set up. No one knew if it could hold.

Meanwhile, to the east near the Chosin Reservoir, the CCF went on the attack against the 1st Marine Division and the 7th Infantry Division. After dark on the night of November 28, in subzero weather and amid swirling snow, the CCF launched heavy attacks from both the front and the flanks. The battle was one of the most brutal that Americans had ever encountered, in this or any other war. East of Chosin, Task Force McLean/Faith was virtually annihilated. Only 385 soldiers of its 3,200-man force reached friendly lines. When McLean was lost, Faith assumed command. Neither man survived.

The 5th and 7th Marine Regiments, against fearful odds, loaded their dead and wounded on trucks and began a fighting retreat (6–49 to 6–51). Oliver Smith concentrated his Marines, and the remnants of Task Force Faith at Hagaru-ri, near a crucial airstrip, where supplies and ammunition were flown in, and some 4,300 wounded were evacuated by air (6–52 and 6–53). By December 7, the Marine column was at Koto-ri, along with a few

6–53 Walking wounded await evacuation from Hagaru-ri.

6–54 Military installations burn as Wonsan is evacuated.

6–55 Thousands of terror-stricken Koreans move south.

6–56 Friendly North Koreans volunteer to aid the South as guerrilla fighters.

U.S. Army, Royal Marine, and ROK units. South of Koto-ri, a crucial bridge had been blown, but the Air Force dropped spans of a treadway bridge that the Marines, often under heavy fire, managed to wrestle into place. This epic ordeal lasted thirteen days, but the Marines came out with their dead, their wounded, and their equipment.

By this time, all of X Corps was pulling back and preparing to cut its losses, leave North Korea, and admit defeat. The U.S. Navy achieved a massive, almost incred-ible, evacuation and did itself proud. Loading first began at Wonsan. Some supplies were destroyed (6–54), but most were loaded on board Navy ships, along with military people, vehi-cles, and equipment. Then came a horde of civilians, pleading to be evacuated (6–55). Among the civilians were hundreds of friendly guerrillas anxious to serve the UN effort (6–56). Although some seven thousand civilians boarded the ships, three times that many had to be left behind for lack of room. On the west coast at Chinnampo, another evacuation was taking place. As the Chinese drew closer, a destroyer task force consisting of Canadian, Australian, and Ameri-can vessels, managed to bring out nearly eight thousand military personnel and civilians.

The greatest sealift took place at Hungnam, where an arc-shaped defensive perimeter was estab-lished, then slowly contracted. The order of evacuation was 1st Marines, ROK units, 7th Infantry Division, and 3d Infantry Division. The last of the soldiers loaded out

6–57 Vehicles being loaded on board ships during the withdrawal from Hungnam.

6–58 Troops of the 7th Regiment, 3d Infantry Division, wading through icy water as they evacuate the beaches.

6–59 Desperate refugees use anything that will float to evacuate Hungnam.

6–60 General Smith pays homage to the fallen members of his 1st Marine Division before departing from Hungnam.

on Christmas Eve, and none of them was sorry to leave (6–57 to 6–60). Once again, thousands of refugees begged to be brought along, and the Navy managed to load ninety-one thousand of them, nearly as many civilians as troops. Admiral Doyle, who directed the operation, said rue-fully that if there were enough time and enough shipping, all of eastern North Korea might have been depopulated. Even as demolitions were going off in the port area, civilians were still trudging into the city.

In the Eighth Army sector, the CCF had outflanked the shaky line south of Pyongyang. Again, Eighth Army troops, tired, cold, and dispirited, were forced to withdraw. By year's end, they were digging in along the 38th Parallel, and they also had a new commander. The tough cavalryman,

6–61 Docks at Hungnam being destroyed by UN forces.

6–62 Lt. Gen. Walton H. Walker just before his death.

6–63 This truck from the 6th ROK Division collided with General Walker's jeep. The accident resulted in the general's death.

Walton Walker, who had led the Eighth Army ably in both triumph and defeat, had been killed instantly when his jeep collided with an ROK truck on December 23, 1950 (6–62 and 6–63). It was announced in Washington that Walker's replacement would be the famed World War II paratrooper, Lt. Gen. Matthew B. Ridgway (6–64).

6–64 Lt. Gen. Matthew B. Ridgway.

⊣SEVEN⊢
The New War

Lt. Gen. Matthew B. Ridgway, the new Eighth Army commander, had his work cut out for him (7–1). In his memoir of the Korean War, he later wrote that "the spirit of the Eighth Army as I found it on my arrival there gave me deep concern. There was a definite air of nervousness, of gloomy foreboding, of uncertainty, a spirit of apprehension as to what the future held." (7–2)

During the next few weeks, the fifty-five-year-old Ridgway turned the dispirited Eighth Army into a dynamic fighting force. His effort stands as one of the great leadership feats in American history. Setting the example himself, Ridgway was constantly on the go—talking to the troops, hearing their problems, and doing everything in his power to solve the problems. "You will have my utmost," he told them, "I shall expect yours." Soon, everyone knew of Ridgway's fighting spirit, exemplified by the trademark grenade attached to his shoulder harness. He exuded a feeling of confidence, and the troops responded (7–3 and 7–4). "The issue now joined in Korea," he told them, "is whether Communism or individual freedom shall prevail; whether the flight of fear-driven people we have witnessed here shall be checked, or shall at

7–1 Lt. Gen. Matthew B. Ridgway (right) assumes command of the Eighth Army. Here, on December 26, 1950, he is greeted by Maj. Gen. Levan G. Allen, Chief of Staff.

7–2 Elements of the 3d Infantry Division fall back from Osan.

some future time, however distant, engulf our own loved ones in all its misery and despair. . . ."

Ridgway told his staff that he had little interest in their defense plans; he wanted to hear their plans for attack. At the moment, however, the weakened Eighth Army was incapable of mounting an attack. The Chinese still had the momentum, and, on New Year's Eve, launched their third-phase offensive that aimed, as usual, at the shaky ROK divisions. When the 6th ROK Division gave way, units on the flank were unable to hold and the rout was on (7–5 and 7–6). With the line broken in several places, Ridgway was forced to order a withdrawal. This meant abandoning Seoul, and the roads were again jammed with fleeing refugees (7–7 and

7–3 General Ridgway (right) doing some hands-on planning with an officer at the front.

7–8). The army fell back to a line south of the Han River that ran roughly along the 37th Parallel. Fortunately, the pressure let up after a week or so. With the U.S. Air Force constantly attacking its supply lines and making move-

7–4 General Ridgway (second from left) is briefed at a 19th Infantry Regiment observation post.

ment during the day almost impossible, the enemy had to rely on what troops could carry on their persons (7–9 and 7–10). After a week, they had to hold up and wait for resupply.

Some of the commanders whom Ridgway inherited were ineffective; others were simply worn out. One by one, he brought in his own people to replace them, and he instilled in them his

7–5 Men of the 19th Infantry Regiment, 24th Division, in retreat ten miles south of Seoul.

7–6 A bridge over the Han River is blown as the last UN forces retreat from Seoul.

7–7 With bridges blown, refugees are forced to flee across the frozen Han River.

own aggressive spirit. Among the newcomers were Maj. Gen. Claude B. ("Buddy") Ferenbaugh, who assumed command of the 7th Division; Maj. Gen. Blackshear M. ("Babe") Bryan, Ridgway's former chief of staff in the Caribbean Command, who became the new commander of the 24th Division; and Maj. Gen. Bryant E. Moore, a former West Point superintendent, who took over for Maj. Gen. John B. Coulter at IX Corps (7–11 to 7–14). Ridgway told his generals to get out of their command posts and spend time with frontline troops. In addition, he wanted them to use patrols to reestablish contact with the CCF and maintain it with a "bulldog grip."

Suddenly, pilots reported that the enemy seemed to be moving north. Ridgway was happy to hear it, as was visiting Army Chief of Staff J. Lawton Collins (7–15). If the enemy was backing off, fine. The UN would be right behind it. The goal, however, was not territorial gain but causing maximum pain for the enemy. In Ridgway's opinion, which was shared by Washington, conquering all of

7–8 Citizens fleeing in the snow.

7–9 A B-26 Invader rains flames of destruction on North Korean targets below.

7–10 A B-29 Superfortress crew makes ready for a mission over North Korea.

7–11 General Ridgway (left) chatting with Maj. Gen. Claude B. Ferenbaugh, Commander, 7th Division.

7–12 Maj. Gen. Blackshear M. ("Babe") Bryan, the new commanding general of the 24th Division.

7–13 Maj. Gen. Bryant E. Moore, Commander, IX Corps.

7–14 Maj. Gen. John B. Coulter (right) talking with General Ridgway prior to Coulter's departure as IX Corps commander.

7–15 Gen. J. Lawton Collins (left) accompanied by Lt. Gen. Ridgway (center) is greeted by Maj. Gen. Frank W. Milburn, Commanding General, I Corps.

7–16 April 3, 1951. General MacArthur (right) is greeted by General Ridgway (left).

North Korea was no longer in the cards, particularly because an effort to do so might trigger a war with either China or the Soviet Union. The war would end only when the enemy decided that it had had enough and that it was too costly to continue.

Operation Thunderbolt, launched by IX Corps and I Corps on January 25, 1951, pushed the CCF back north of the Han River. A pleased Douglas MacArthur arrived on January 28 to visit the front and to confer with Ridgway (7–16 and 7–17). On the eastern

7–17 Generals MacArthur (center front) and Ridgway (right front) survey the situation at the front.

7–19 Tanks move into position for direct fire as men of the 25th Infantry Division dig in near Suwon.

7–18 Members of the 27th Infantry Regiment, 25th Division, move forward. They pay little heed to a dead North Korean soldier disguised as a civilian.

7–20 Men of the 27th Infantry Regiment and M-46 tanks of the 64th Tank Battalion forge ahead 10 miles southwest of Seoul.

7–21 A medic tending to the wounds of an American GI.

7–22 Sgt. Mike Chalooga of Honolulu, Hawaii, examines a dead North Korean soldier who was carrying an American short-story magazine.

7–23 General Ridgway (left) and Maj. Gen. Charles D. Palmer, Commanding General, 1st Cavalry Division, discuss the Chipyong-ni situation.

7–24 General Ridgway (at microphone) addresses French forces during a ceremony at which they are awarded a battle streamer for their actions at Chipyong-ni.

front, X Corps and the ROK III Corps began Operation Roundup (7–18 to 7–22). This time, the enemy fought back fiercely as it launched what it called its fourth-phase offensive. At Chipyong-ni northwest of Wonju on X Corps's right flank, the 23d Infantry Regiment of Maj. Gen. Clark Ruffner's 2d Infantry Division and the French Battalion, plus supporting tanks and artillery, were surrounded for several days by elements of six CCF divisions. After three days of intensive fighting, a task force from the 1st Cavalry Division, in a controversial, costly operation, broke through to lift the siege. It had been an epic battle, and, despite all-out assaults during which four CCF divisions were shattered, the enemy had failed to overrun the perimeter (7–23 to 7–25).

The Air Force continued to pound enemy supply lines, and, in order to restrict supply by sea, the Navy's Task Force 95 began an

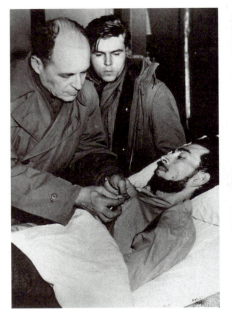

7–25 General Ridgway presents a Silver Star to 1st Lt. Pierre Laniel, a French officer wounded in action.

7–26 The USS *Lind* shells targets from her position in Wonsan harbor.

7–27 Smoke and flames rise in the air after U.S. Air Force planes drop bombs on bridges over the Han River.

effective blockade of Wonsan harbor, one that would continue to the war's end (7–26).

On February 21, another Eighth Army offensive, Operation Killer, was under way. The name bothered a few Washington bureaucrats. What would the public think? In his memoirs, Ridgway said that it was a good idea to remind people that war was about killing; maybe if they *were* reminded, they would be more reluctant to get involved in one. Next, on March 7, Operation Ripper began with an advance across the Han River by I and X Corps (7–27). CCF casualties continued to mount. Not only were the Chinese being hammered by constant air strikes and devastating artillery barrages, they were now increasingly weakened by hunger and disease (7–28 to 7–31).

7–28 Men of the 545th Military Police Company, 1st Cavalry Division, bring in three Chinese prisoners.

Tragically, on February 24, the IX Corps Commander, Bryant E. Moore, died of a heart attack after the helicopter in which he was riding struck a cable and plunged him into the icy Han River (7–32 and 7–33). His replacement was fifty-seven-year-old Maj. Gen.

7–29 GIs remove a dead enemy soldier from railroad tracks.

7–30 Marines capture Chinese prisoners at Hoensong.

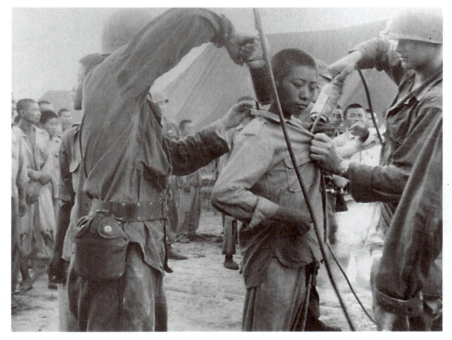

7–31 North Korean POW being deloused by Cpl. Kenneth White (right) of Grand Junction, Colorado, and Pfc. Carol Cutting of Kezar Falls, Maine.

William M. Hoge, a hard-nosed fighter (7–34). During World War II, Hoge had led a brigade of combat engineers onto Omaha Beach on D-Day. Pending Hoge's arrival, Ridgway gave temporary command of IX Corps to Marine General Oliver P. Smith.

UN forces recaptured Seoul from the enemy on March 14. It was the fourth (and final) time that the South Korean capital had changed hands. Soon after, on March 23, the 187th Airborne RCT dropped on Munsan-ni, 20 miles north of Seoul. Although the airdrop failed to trap large numbers of enemy soldiers, it contributed to the overall advance. By the end of March,

7–32 Maj. Gen. Bryant E. Moore. Authorized a third star, he did not live long enough to receive it.

7–33 General Moore's casket being loaded on an airplane for its journey home.

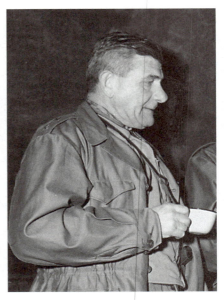

7–34 Maj. Gen. William M. Hoge, the new commanding general of IX Corps.

7–35 Men of the 25th Infantry Division direct artillery fire near the 38th Parallel.

7–36 Paratroopers of the 187th Regimental Combat Team jump from C-119s near Munsan-ni.

the UN forces were once more at the 38th Parallel (7–35 to 7–39).

On April 3, Ridgway met with General MacArthur, who flew from Tokyo for a conference (7–40). Ridgway explained his plan, which was to use his air and artillery support to inflict maximum casualties on the enemy while minimizing his own. Accordingly, he would advance,

slowly and deliberately, to a series of phase lines named Kansas, Wyoming, and Utah. This would bring him to the vicinity of Chorwon, Pyongyang, and Kumhwa, a strategically important area known as the Iron Triangle.

For months, President Truman had been growing increasingly annoyed with MacArthur, who obviously did not agree with the

Administration's policy of limited war. On March 24, MacArthur issued a public statement taunting China in almost arrogant terms; offering to meet with the Chinese to negotiate an end to the war; and saying, as an implied threat, that if the UN chose to extend the war to the Chinese homeland, the

7–37 Paratroopers float toward earth near Munsan-ni.

7–38 Pinned down by enemy fire, men of the 3d Infantry Division take cover.

7–39 SFC D. C. Miller of Avon, New York (right), erects a sign on the 38th Parallel to mark the 2d Infantry Division's second crossing into North Korea.

7–40 Leaving Kimpo Air Force Base for an inspection tour are (left to right) General Ridgway, Maj. Gen. Doyle O. Hickey, Eighth Army, General MacArthur, and a driver.

Chinese regime would certainly collapse. Four days earlier, to make matters worse, MacArthur had written to Republican Congressman Joseph Martin: "We must win [in Asia], there is no substitute for victory."

That did it. With the concurrence of the Joint Chiefs and the State Department, Truman decided to fire the legendary Douglas MacArthur and replace him with Ridgway. The plan was for MacArthur to be informed of the firing by Secretary of the Army Frank Pace, who was then on a tour of the Far East (7–41). Because of a communications foul-up, by the time that Eighth Army Chief of Staff Leven C. ("Lev") Allen had relayed the message to Pace, MacArthur had already heard the news over the radio. The way it was done, as much as the firing itself, caused a public outcry. MacArthur returned to the States, where he was hailed as a hero and honored in a series of parades and personal appearances (7–42). His most famous appearance was before the U.S. Congress, where he gave a stirring, emotional speech that ended with a quote from an old barracks-room ballad: "Old soldiers never die, they just fade away."

7–41 Secretary of the Army Frank Pace.

7–42 General MacArthur waves during a New York City ticker tape parade. With him is New York Mayor Vincent Impellitteri.

The new Eighth Army commander, replacing Ridgway, was Lt. Gen. James A. Van Fleet. The fifty-nine-year-old Van Fleet, a decorated combat veteran of both World Wars, had led his regiment ashore at Utah Beach on D-Day and, later in the war, had commanded the U.S. Army's III Corps in its breakout from the Remagen bridgehead and advance into Austria (7–43).

On April 22, the CCF launched its fifth-phase spring offensive. Some 250,000 men in twenty-seven divisions hit the UN line along a 40-mile front north of Seoul. In one historic encounter near Kapyong, the 1st Battalion of the Gloucestershire Regiment was decimated after holding off the Chinese for sixty crucial hours, which had significantly slowed the momentum of the enemy offensive. Van Fleet called the battalion's action, with no exaggeration, "the most outstanding

7–43 New Eighth Army commander, Lt. Gen. James A. Van Fleet (second from left) arrives at the 24th Division's airstrip. Saluting is 24th Division Chief of Staff Col. Charles S. O'Malley. Hidden behind O'Malley is General Bryan, Commander, 24th Infantry Division. At far left is Bryan's aide-de-camp, Lt. Harry J. Maihafer.

example of unit bravery in modern warfare."

The Chinese, seemingly oblivious to the cost in human bodies, continued their mass attacks.

Time Magazine quoted one officer: "They attack, and we shoot them down. Then we pull back, and they have to do it all over again. . . . They're spending people the way we spend ammunition." By the time the CCF spring offensive, its greatest of war, had run its course, the enemy had suffered an incredible seventy thousand casualties (7–44, 7–45). Moreover, the Chinese had failed to attain their primary objective, the capture of Seoul.

In mid-May, the enemy launched still another attack, this time with twenty-one Chinese and nine North Korean divisions, in an all-out effort—it would either wipe out the UN forces completely or drive them off the peninsula altogether. Once again, after suffering heavy losses, the enemy offensive shuddered to a halt. At this point, with the enemy overextended, Van Fleet mounted his own attack, gained ground, overran enemy supply points, and inflicted still more casualties. Some correspondents called it the "May massacre." Meanwhile, the Air Force had launched Operation Strangle, an air interdiction campaign, and U.S. Air Force Capt. James Jabara, flying an F-86 Sabrejet, had become the first jet air ace in history (7–46 and 7–47).

The Eighth Army offensive continued into June, with I and IX Corps advancing toward Line Wyoming in the Iron Triangle area. They could have kept going, but for political reasons, complete victory was no longer an option and there seemed little point in shedding more blood. All of the major participants (with the possible exception of Syngman Rhee) now recognized that the war was

7–44 A Chinese POW.

7–45 More Chinese prisoners. From the looks on their faces, they are being treated well.

7–46 Results of a B-29 raid on the Pyongyang rail yard.

not going to be "won," in the normal sense of the word. Perhaps, in fact, the Chinese might now find the cost of carrying on the war too high in casualties and equipment and be more receptive to negotiations.

In early June, Trygve Lie, Secretary General of the United Nations, proffered another peace bid. Then on June 23, following secret diplomatic initiatives by the Americans, the Soviet UN delegate, Jacob Malik, proposed ceasefire discussions. A week later, on orders from Washington, General Ridgway announced that the UN was willing to discuss an armistice. In response, Marshal Kim Il Sung, commander of the NKPA, and Peng Teh-huai, CCF commander, agreed to begin talks.

On July 10, 1951, a UN team headed by Adm. C. Turner Joy met with NKPA and CCF delegates at Kaesong (7–48 and 7–49). Senior U.S. Army and Air Force representatives, respectively, were Maj. Gen. Henry I. Hodes, Deputy Chief of Staff, Eighth Army; and Maj. Gen. Laurence C. Craigie, Vice Commander, Far East Air Forces. The senior ROK delegate was Gen. Paik

7–47 An F-86 Sabrejet, America's fastest fighter at the time.

7–48 Vice Adm. C. Turner Joy, senior U.S. military advisor in Korea.

7–49 Kaesong conference site, where the first phase of the military armistice negotiations began in July 1951.

7–50 UN delegates on their way to the negotiations at Kaesong. Left to right in backseat of the jeep are Maj. Gen. Laurence C. Craigie, Vice Commander, Far Eastern Air Forces, and Maj.Gen. Paik Sun Yup, Commanding General, 1st ROK Corps. Vice Adm. C. Turner Joy, Commander, Naval Forces, Far East, is in the front passenger seat.

7–51 Admiral Joy (left) and Maj. Gen. Henry I. Hodes, leaving for chow, pass a North Korean guard along the way.

Sun Yup, who had successfully commanded ROK I Corps (7–50 and 7–51). Senior communist delegates were North Korean Gen. Nam Il and Chinese Gen. Peng Teh-huai. Nam Il, although only in his late thirties, was chief of staff of the NKPA and also vice premier of North Korea. Educated in Manchuria, he spoke Chinese and Russian in addition to Korean (7–52 and 7–53).

Almost immediately, the talks ran into trouble. The communists seemed intent not only on "saving face" but on portraying themselves as victors. On the night of July 10, UN newsmen set up a betting pool on the length of the armistice negotiations. The pessimists guessed that it would take six weeks. As it turned out, a fortnight passed before the conferees could reach agreement on the

7–52 Communist delegation at the Kaesong armistice meeting. North Korean Gen. Nam Il is in the center.

7–53 Communist soldiers stand outside the conference room during a break in the armistice sessions at Kaesong.

7–54 Men of the 7th Infantry Regiment, 3d Division, camouflage their foxholes in the Kagae-dong area.

7–55 UN troops moving up Hill 717.

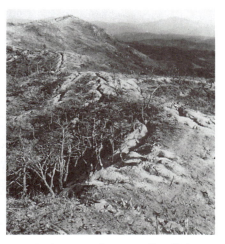

7–56 A general view of Hill 346 that shows enemy communication trenches from bunker to bunker.

agenda alone. On August 5, the United Nations Command (UNC) suspended the talks because communist armed troops were present in the neutral area. On August 10, the talks were resumed, only to be halted again on August 22 because of violations of the neutral area by UN aircraft.

With the talks suspended, the fighting resumed with new intensity. The Americans, South Koreans, and UN Allies fought and died at formerly obscure pieces of Korean real estate, places now made famous with such names as Bloody Ridge, Heartbreak Ridge, and Old Baldy (7–54 to 7–57).

Finally, after weeks of delay, the truce talks resumed on October 25. Negotiators had agreed to move the talks from Kaesong to Panmunjom. The end seemed to be in sight. At this point, no one foresaw that the war was less than half over.

7–57 Patrolling Marines take a break. As negotiations dragged on, men continued to fight and die.

EIGHT

The Tools of War

8–1 Enemy T-34 tank put out of action by a mine.

Some historians call Korea the "Forgotten War," which is not completely true. At the very least, however, memories have grown fuzzy, remote, and even unreal. Because Americans can no longer hear the exploding mortar rounds,

8–2 The wreckage of a tank that was caught on a bridge by planes of the U.S. Air Force.

8–3 The 3.5-inch bazooka, a very effective antitank weapon.

8–4 North Korean soldiers, carrying burp guns, execute a change of guard at Kaesong.

the rippling buzz of enemy sub-machine guns, or the high-pitched scream of incoming artillery, it is hard for some people to imagine what the war was like. By seeing some of the tools that men used to wage that war, however, one can at least bring reality a little closer.

The Korean War had come on the heels of World War II, separated from the latter by less than five full years. In the beginning, therefore, it was fought mainly with "leftover" World War II weapons. At the beginning, the South Koreans and the Americans had only light tanks because they believed that these tanks were best suited for the Far East. The communists, on the other hand, knew that the heavier medium tanks, even though roadbound, could be effective in Korea. They spearheaded the war's opening drive with Soviet-made T-34s mounting powerful 85-mm cannons (8–1). Although the T-34s seemed invincible at first, aerial rockets, mines, and 3.5-inch bazookas, later proved highly effective against them (8–2 and 8–3).

Communist Forces

The NKPA was equipped almost entirely with Soviet-supplied weapons of World War II vintage. Most communist foot soldiers, both North Korean and Chinese, were armed with the 7.62-mm submachine gun. Because of its rapid-fire, murmuring sound, GIs called it a "burp gun" (8–4). Ground troops also used either Soviet or Japanese rifles (8–5), handguns, and a variety of

8–5 A standard .31-caliber rifle used by communist forces.

8–6 Wheel-carriage–mounted machine gun.

8–7 Another type of mounted machine gun used by the communist forces.

machine guns. Many of the machine guns, unlike their American counterparts, were on wheeled carriages (8–6 and 8–7). Although the Soviets supplied nearly all of the NKPA weaponry, it was not always of Soviet manufacture. Some was captured German or Japanese equipment from World War II or made in Soviet-bloc countries, such as Czechoslovakia. The captured Bren gun in photograph 8–8 was of British origin.

8–8 A captured Bren gun.

The North Koreans and Chinese made good use of mortars (8–9) and also employed a wide variety of antitank and antiaircraft weapons. Heavy artillery was sel-dom seen during the early days of the war, but the 150-mm howitzer came into play after the entry of China. Unlike American artillery, which stressed mobility, Chinese howitzers were often dug in at fixed locations and, to provide concealment, frequently emplaced in large earthen dugouts (8–10 and 8–11).

The variety of communist weaponry, both in caliber and in country of origin, often presented logistical problems, particularly with regard to ammunition. Similarly, the hodgepodge of vehicles, including various models of self-propelled guns, Soviet-made jeeps, "Molotov" trucks, and even armored cars, created severe maintenance problems for countries where the average fighting man had little or no mechanical background (8–12).

At the beginning of the war, the North Korean Air Force had about 180 Soviet-made airplanes, all propeller driven, and many of them were nearly obsolete. The best of these were the 40 Yakolev (Yak) fighter planes, effective early in the war for strafing airfields and infantry formations and, on occasion, attacking flights of U.S. bombers (8–13). By mid-summer of 1950, however, the U.S. Navy and the U.S. Air Force had virtually destroyed the North Korean Air Force, and, for the remainder of the war, the United States had virtual air supremacy over all of Korea.

Beginning in November of 1950, the CCF Air Force entered the war, represented mainly by squadrons of MiG 15s, often flown by Soviet pilots in an area that became known as "MiG Alley." The MiGs operated from Manchurian air bases on the far side of the Yalu River, "sanctuaries" that, for political reasons, were off-limits to attack. (8–14)

8–9 A Soviet 120-mm mortar used by the North Korean People's Army.

8–10 A Chinese howitzer.

8–11 Another Chinese howitzer.

8–12 A Soviet-made armored car.

8–13 Capt. Wayne Crawford of Jackson, Michigan, inspects the cockpit of a captured North Korean Yak fighter.

8–14 A captured MiG-15, its markings masked by military censors.

8–15 Pvt. Leonard Wensel of South River, New Jersey, with his M-1 Garand rifle, takes a break.

8–16 A platoon of the 3d Infantry Division advances against a ridge on Hill 717. The men are armed with rifles, carbines, and BARs.

UN Forces

Like the enemy, U.S. and UN foot soldiers entered the war with weapons of World War II vintage. They included the trusty M-1 Garand rifle, the .30-caliber carbine, the Browning automatic rifle (BAR), the .45-caliber pistol (which dated back to before World War I), and light and heavy .30-caliber machine guns (8–15 to 8–18).

In addition, there were the antitank rocket launchers, or

8–17 SFC Major Cleveland (left), weapons squad leader, points out an enemy position to his machine-gun crew.

8–18 Machine-gun crew at an observation post.

8–19 Two soldiers firing a 60-mm mortar.

8–20 57-mm recoilless rifle team in action.

8–21 Soldier firing a recoilless rifle.

bazookas. When the smaller of these, the 2.36-inch, proved to be ineffective, it was replaced by the 3.5-inch model. Other weapons were hand grenades, both fragmentation and white phosphorus, plus 60-mm, 81-mm, and 4.2-inch mortars (8–19). Direct fire support also came from recoilless rifles, 57-mm, 75-mm, and 105-mm (8–20 and 8–21).

Organic American artillery was primarily 105-mm, 155-mm, and 8-inch (8–22 and 8–23). The ROK units had their own 75-mm

artillery batteries, but ROK divisions were normally supported by heavier-caliber U.S. artillery units.

Early in the war, the only U.S. tank was the light M-24 General Chaffee mounting an ineffectual 75-mm gun (8–24). Within the next weeks and months, other tank units were rushed into battle; some had the M4A3E8 Sherman mounting a 76-mm gun (8–25) that could compete with the Soviet-made T-34. Other tank units had the M-26 Pershing (90-mm gun) (8–26) or, later, the

newer M-46 Patton (8–27). Still another tank, the Centurian, was used by the British forces.

A Korean War innovation was the extensive use of helicopters, both for transportation and medical evacuation (8–28). In addition, the Army made good use of light aircraft for transportation and aerial observation (8–29).

Military engineers proved their adaptability. Especially in the early days, they were called on to serve as combat forces. As the war progressed, they demonstrated their

8–22 A 105-mm howitzer being fired by members of the 99th Field Artillery Battalion.

8–23 At dusk, artillerymen of the 11th Field Artillery Battalion, 24th Infantry Division, fire 155-mm howitzers.

8–24 The M-24 General Chaffee light tank.

8–25 An M-4 Sherman tank uses a flamethrower on a Chinese pillbox near the Han River.

8–26 An M-26 Pershing tank moves into position.

8–27 An M-46 Patton tank, carrying troops of the 25th Infantry Division, forges ahead.

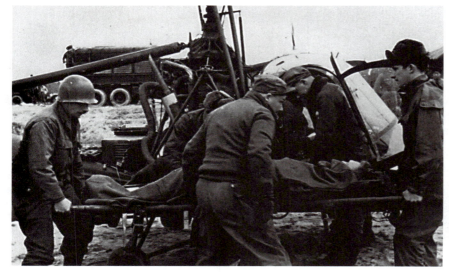

8–28 A wounded soldier is reassured by medics who carry him away from a helicopter medevac.

8–29 A 7th Division L-5E Sentinel aircraft is refueled by Cpl. Charles Morehead of Sherman, West Virginia.

8–30 Northwest of Taegu, vehicles cross a pontoon bridge erected by the 8th Combat Engineer Battalion.

8–31 Troops utilize footbridges as tables for their chow.

8–32 A minesweeping team from the 3d Combat Engineer Battalion locates and clears mines from a road.

8–33 A transmitter and receiver station erected by the 13th Signal Company, 1st Cavalry Division, on a mountaintop near Kaesong.

8–34 A supply area for vehicle parts belonging to the 27th Ordnance Company, 24th Infantry Division.

8–35 Ammunition dump no. 66 located in South Korea.

8–36 The USS *Antietam* under way off the East coast of Korea with Task Force 77.

8–37 U.S. Navy F-2 fighters launch from the deck of the USS *Lake Champlain*.

8–38 The USS *Iowa* fires her 16-inch guns at enemy targets.

8–39 An A-1 Skyraider returns to the USS *Bon Homme Richard* after a mission.

ingenuity in building bridges, and revetments, laying minefields, and performing many other tasks. No one could have worked without the support of service units that provided communication, maintenance, supplies, and ammunition (8–30 to 8–35).

Of course, the Navy and Marines played crucial roles in the war. Not only did the Marines provide ground combat strength but Marine air groups, with their carrier-based F-4U Corsairs, were especially effective. The Navy, providing air and naval gunfire support and controlling the sea lanes with the destroyers, cruisers, and carriers of Task Force 77, wrote a proud page in naval history (8–36 to 8–39).

In addition to the propeller-driven F-51 Mustangs, B-26 Marauders, and B-29 Superfortresses, all veterans of World War II (8–40 to 8–42). Korea saw the introduction of jet aircraft, notably the F-80 Shooting Star and the F-86 Sabrejet (8–43 and 8–44), as well as the use of

8–40 American, Australian, and South Korean aircraft at an airstrip near Taegu.

huge new cargo planes, such as the C-124 Globemaster (8–45). Throughout the war, the United States maintained air superiority, which made life hellish for communist forces; denied them open movement during daylight hours; disrupted their supply lines; and, perhaps worst of all, threatened them with the war's most dreaded tool, the ghastly flaming napalm.

8–41 In a tight formation, B-26 Invaders head for their home base in Japan after a mission over North Korea. The aircraft carried .50-caliber cannons and napalm bombs.

8–42 A formation of B-29s dropping bombs over North Korea.

8–43 Laden with 500-pound high-explosive bombs, U.S. Air Force F-80 Shooting Stars fly toward the front.

8–44 F-86 Sabrejets patrol MiG Alley in northwestern Korea.

8–45 A C-124 Globemaster, the largest transport plane of its day.

⊣NINE⊢

The Static War

As 1952 began, the battle line had more or less stabilized. Nevertheless, men continued to fight—and to die. Mobile army surgical hospital (MASH) units continued to be busy. Unlike the happy-go-lucky people of the popular TV series, *MASH*, the real-life doctors and nurses, as well as the helicopter pilots who flew rescue missions, were facing life-and-death situations on a daily basis. The thousands of men, including one of the authors, who were treated at these MASH units will be forever grateful (9–1 to 9–4).

The front lines, with bunkers, barbed wire, revetments, and sandbagged trenches, began to resemble pictures of World War I battlefields. Attacks were now mostly against limited objectives, and each gain, even for a small piece of ground, came with a terrible price tag (9–5 and 9–6).

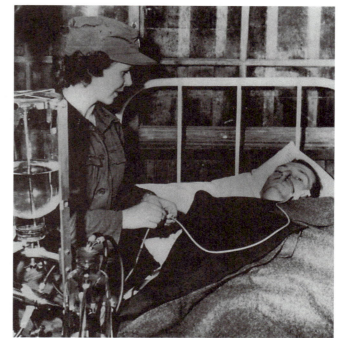

9–1 Nurse Lt. Loraine Williams tends to a patient at the 121st Evacuation Hospital, Yongdong-po.

9–2 Lt. Gen. Matthew B. Ridgway presents the Bronze Star to Maj. Bernice Coleman, Chief Nurse, 1st MASH, for her outstanding service in the care and treatment of wounded men.

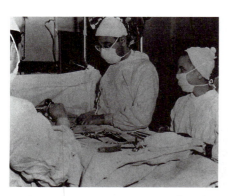

9–3 Capt. Don Artuso, with 2d Lt. Kathryne Polesky in a MASH unit somewhere in Korea.

9–4 A "real" MASH—the 8225th.

9–5 Lt. Ralph Barnes, Company C, 15th Infantry Regiment, throws a hand grenade toward a Chinese position near Uijongbu.

Even when things were at a lull, the pressure was there. The enemy was nearby, often with direct observation, and people learned to walk warily, often crouching to maintain a low profile (9–7).

By this time, a rotation system had been established for both units and individuals. The 1st Cavalry Division was back in Japan. So was the 24th Infantry Division, less the 5th Infantry Regiment and the 555th Field Artillery Battalion, which remained in Korea as the 5th RCT. The newly arrived 40th Infantry Division, now online, had replaced the 24th Division.

Men began calculating their points toward rotation. Those in a frontline unit received four points per month, others less. USO troupes provided a welcome break, as did the service clubs that began to spring up in some of the rear areas (9–8 to 9–10). Even better were the five-day R and R (rest and relaxation) trips to Japan. The mind-set, however,

9–6 Mortar firing from a built-up position. Note sandbags and fortified bunker.

9–8 A USO group performs for the 24th Infantry Division.

9–7 A reading of caution in front of the Hantan River bridge on Road 3 near Kumhwa. (M.L.R. means "Main Line of Resistance.")

9–9 The war became "official" when Bob Hope, the most active and famous USO entertainer of the twentieth century, arrived to entertain the troops.

had changed from winning the war to ending one's tour and getting home safely.

The talks at Panmunjom, however, dragged on as U.S. and ROK negotiators continually faced communist intransigence. UN representatives believed that the talks should be military in character, with a goal of ending the war. Therefore, Admiral Joy's team was being pressed to wind up the negotiations as quickly as possible. On the other hand, the communists, who were using the talks for propaganda purposes, were in no hurry. They were quite willing to trade manpower indefinitely with the Americans and the South Koreans. Sadly enough, the side that placed little value on the worth of the individual had a built-in advantage. To keep the pressure on, Ridgway and Van Fleet decided that fighting should continue while the talks were in progress. Although this turned out to be the right decision, for the men doing the fighting, as well as for the American public, it seemed wrong to take casualties when there was no plan for all-out victory (9–11 and 9–12).

After prisoner lists were exchanged, the UN proposed a voluntary exchange of POWs. Many enemy prisoners, perhaps fearing retribution, refused repatriation. The Chinese and North Koreans insisted that *all* POWs be exchanged and refused to change their position. Once more, talks were at a stalemate. To complicate matters, communist-inspired riots broke out at the Koje-do prison

9–10 Soldiers enjoying refreshments at the Masan Service Club.

9–11 Chinese and North Korean delegates leaving a conference.

camp, and, embarrassingly, Chinese and North Korean prisoners actually controlled the camp for a considerable time (9–13 to 9–15). Next, the communists charged that the UN was using germ warfare. This was vigorously denied, and international observers offered to go to North Korea to

9–12 After a frustrating day with no agreement reached between the two factions, Lt. Gen. Matthew B. Ridgway leaves the conference tent.

investigate the charge. When access was denied, and even the Soviet UN delegate remained silent on the question, the phoniness of the charge became evident. Even today, however, Kim Il Sung's official biography repeats the "germ warfare" hoax as gospel.

In May of 1952, Lt. Gen. Mark W. Clark replaced Ridgway as head of Far East Command and as commander-in-chief, United Nations Command. Fifty-six-year-old Clark, a 1917 West Point classmate of Ridgway's, inherited a frustrating mission, waging a war of limited objectives with no clear end in sight (9–16). The aggressive Clark might have favored a major ground offensive, but, according to the higher-ups, that was not an option.

As an alternative and a means of maintaining pressure on the enemy, the air campaign became even more intense. The U.S. Navy and the U.S. Air Force, flying from South Korean airfields or off carriers, continued to inflict heavy damage as they waged a successful interdiction campaign and attacked such key targets as hydroelectric plants. By this time, the enemy had hundreds of MiG fighters, sallying forth at will, that usually avoided the F-86 Sabrejets and went after the slower F-80s and F-84s. After engagement, the MiGs then scurried back to their bases north of the Yalu. In a remarkable performance, and despite the disadvantage imposed by these sanctuaries, UN fliers did the job and maintained air superiority throughout the war. In the

long run, this air campaign, which severely hurt the enemy but incurred relatively few friendly casualties, became a decisive factor in the peace negotiations (9–17 to 9–20).

As the truce talks dragged on at Panmunjom, Maj. Gen. William K. Harrison, Jr., replaced Admiral

9–13 Homemade Chinese weapons confiscated during riots at POW camp no. 10 on May 20, 1952. The weapons were made from bedposts, tent poles, and any objects that could be sharpened.

Joy as chief UN negotiator. Throughout the summer, vicious, bitter, localized fighting took place along the battle line. Hills with such names as Old Baldy, Pork Chop, Jane Russell, White Horse, and Pike's Peak were entering the proud pages of American history (9–21). That August, the

9–14 A Communist POW verbally abuses a U.S. Army major at a prisoner exchange in Panmunjom.

9–15 Exercising North Korean POWs. Their humane treatment was in sharp contrast to that received by UN prisoners.

U.S. Marines captured Hill 122 east of Panmunjom and gave it the memorable nickname of Bunker Hill.

The communist demand for forcible repatriation of prisoners was still an issue. In October, the UN negotiators, after making significant concessions, issued what was their "final package" of proposals for prisoner exchange and ending the war. Once again, the communists rejected what was offered and did so in insulting terms. At this point, General Harrison and the other UN delegates walked out of the meeting. They declared a recess until the communists were willing to accept one or more of the UN plans or submit in writing a constructive plan of their own (9–22 and 9–23).

In December 1952, President-elect Dwight D. Eisenhower visited Korea, thereby fulfilling one of his campaign promises. He had

9–18 B-26s leave targets at Korangpo-ri in smoke and flames.

9–19 B-29s dropped thousands of tons of bombs on enemy targets during the last days of the war.

9--16 General Ridgway (left) and Lt. Gen. Mark W. Clark discuss strategy just before Ridgway is replaced as commander in chief of the UN command.

9–20 "Esprit de corps." Six African American crewmen of the 917th Bomber Wing join hands before a mission.

9–17 The F-51 Mustang was the last of the great prop fighters.

9–21 GIs dig in at positions on Old Baldy.

9–22 Frustrated UN representatives leave yet another fruitless peace commission meeting.

9–23 UN POW camp at Pusan held both North Korean and Chinese prisoners.

9–24 President-elect Dwight D. Eisenhower (left) and his son, Maj. John Eisenhower, at the Light Air Section, 3d Infantry Division.

9–25 President-elect Eisenhower eats dinner with S/Sgt. Virgil Hutchinson, a squad leader in the 3d Infantry Division.

9–26 Gen. Maxwell D. Taylor.

9–27 Guns of the 937th Field Artillery Battalion fire to break up a communist night attack.

told the American people that he would go to Korea and see for himself what was happening. He visited many units and talked not only to officers (including his son John) but also to enlisted men (9–24). Speaking to a press conference on the last day of his visit, Eisenhower admitted that he had "no panaceas, no tricks" for bringing the war to a close. Significantly, he never once discussed seeking a military victory (9–25).

After taking office in February 1953, Eisenhower named Lt. Gen. Maxwell D. Taylor to replace Van Fleet as Eighth Army commander (9–26). Soon after Taylor's arrival, the Chinese launched massive attacks in the area of Old Baldy, T-Bone, and Pork Chop. The UN defenders, with the maximum use of supporting artillery, made the enemy pay a heavy price (9–27 and 9–28). Taylor, knowing Eisenhower's desires, gave up Old Baldy and Pork Chop rather than order a counterattack. At this point, it made no sense to incur heavy casualties for pieces of obscure real estate.

Truce talks resumed at Panmunjom in March of 1953. The following month, sick and wounded prisoners were exchanged in Operation Little Switch (9–29 and 9–30). In June, perhaps trying to improve its geographic position, the CCF launched massive attacks involving three Chinese armies, almost 100,000 troops. The drive, directed mainly against ROK divisions, gained several thousand yards. It was finally stopped by

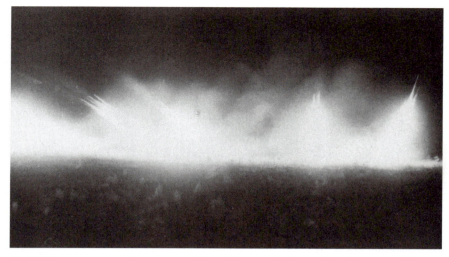

9–28 Impact area during a night of heavy fighting by the 2d Rocket Field Artillery battery in the Chorwon area.

9–29 Maj. Gen. Lee Sang-jo, communist liaison officer at Panmunjom, departs after agreeing to the exchange of sick and wounded POWs.

9–30 UN delegate Rear Adm. John C. Daniel, U.S. Navy (left) and other liaison officers look over the site of the POW exchange (Little Switch) at Panmunjom.

9–31 Gen. William K. Harrison, Jr. (sitting at table on left) and North Korean Gen. Nam Il (sitting at table on right) sign armistice documents to end the three-year Korean conflict.

9–32 A view of the Freedom Tent, the POW exchange point at Freedom Village in Munsan-ni.

9–33 UN POWs are off-loaded from ambulances at Panmunjom.

immense artillery barrages, about 2.7 million rounds in June alone.

In a way, this was a last gasp. On July 10, truce talks resumed. After more discussions, this time serious ones, a cease-fire was signed on July 27, 1953, at Panmunjom. Gen. Nam Il signed for the North Koreans and General Harrison for the UN (9–31). Later that day, General Clark countersigned the document at Munsanni. During the final truce talks ground activity had come to a halt, but artillery and mortar fire had continued until the cease-fire was signed. Also, Air Force, Navy, and Marine aircraft had continued to pound North Korean airfields, rail lines, and road systems. On the sea, naval warships bombarded Kosong and finally ended the longest naval siege in history by shelling Wonsan for the last time.

When he signed the armistice agreement, Clark cautioned that it was only a military decision to stop shooting while the opposing

9–34 Maj. Gen. William F. Dean, former commanding general of the 24th Infantry Division (in dark suit), is repatriated under the terms of the POW exchange (Big Switch) after three years in captivity. He is greeted by General Taylor (left) on his arrival at Freedom Village.

9–35 An anticommunist North Korean just released from a POW camp acts as a cheerleader for other recently released POWs as he waves a South Korean flag.

9–36 A happy reunion on board a C-124 for a released POW. Capt. Zach W. Dean of El Dorado, Kansas, clasps his wife tightly just after the plane lands in Tokyo.

sides sought a political solution to the conflict. Fifty years after the start of the Korean War, that "political solution" has not yet arrived, so technically a state of war still exists. For Mark Clark, it was a bittersweet moment. In his memoirs, he later complained, "In carrying out the instructions of my government, I gained the unenviable distinction of being the first United States Army commander in history to sign an armistice without victory."

From August 5 to September 6, 1953, the final exchange of prisoners, Operation Big Switch, took place at Freedom Village. The communists returned 12,757 prisoners, of whom 7,848 were South Koreans, 1,312 were other UN personnel, and 3,597 were Americans. The UN turned over to the communists a total of 75,823 prisoners, about 70,000 of them North Koreans and the rest Chinese. More than 22,000 civilian detainees, about two thirds of them Chinese, and the rest North

Koreans, refused to be repatriated. According to the agreement, each man was marched into a tent and subjected to a communist harangue, often for several hours, in an attempt to convince him to change his mind. It did not work. Except for a handful, no one altered his decision; most even refused to listen to the so-called "explanations." In many ways, their refusal to return to their communist countries was a convincing victory for the forces of democracy (9–32 to 9–36).

TEN

Aftermath

In June 1950, after authorizing American forces to offer "all possible support" to South Korea, Harry Truman told Secretary of State Dean Acheson, "I've been President five years, and I've spent five years trying to avoid making a decision like the one I've had to make tonight. What I want you to know is that this is not a decision just for Korea. It is a decision for the United Nations itself." History has shown that Harry Truman made the right decision.

Once the UN Security Council approved intervention, the goal of the United States was to secure the support of as many allies as possible. At first, just the Americans helped the Republic of Korea, but combat, support, and

10–1 Syngman Rhee visits the ROK 1st Infantry Division.

medical units from nineteen other UN countries eventually joined the war against North Korea. The units ranged in size from a small battalion of six hundred men to a brigade of six thousand men and totaled more than twenty-eight thousand ground troops.

Any discussion of allies, of course, must start with the gallant

South Koreans and their strong-willed president, Syngman Rhee (10–1). Admittedly, as the war began, the men of the ROK Army were green, untrained, and ill equipped. But, for days, they stood alone, and thousands fought gamely, many to their deaths. U.S. Army Chief of Staff J. Lawton Collins visited Korea in 1951 and

10–2 Gen. J. Lawton Collins, U.S. Army Chief of Staff, decorates South Korean soldiers.

10–3 Australian troops cross the 38th Parallel at Tamuri.

10–4 Members of the Belgian Battalion advance against the Chinese.

10–5 Colombian soldiers walk down the gangplank in Pusan to join UN forces in Korea.

took the time to award decorations to ROK soldiers who had distinguished themselves in battle (10–2).

Although the bulk of the fighting forces would come from either America or South Korea, all contributions were welcomed, regardless of size, both for the military benefit and for the moral impact on the international community. Combat units were furnished by Australia, Belgium/Luxembourg, Canada, Colombia, Ethiopia, France, Greece, the Netherlands, New Zealand, the Philippines, the Republic of South Africa, Thailand, Turkey, and Great Britain (10–3 to 10–7). Medical units

10–6 Pfc. Morris J. Piche of Ottawa, Canada (left), is helped by a fellow Canadian, Lance Cpl. W. J. Chrysler of Hamilton, Ontario.

10–7 Bagpiper leads a platoon of Welsh Highlanders through the IX Corps area.

were furnished by Denmark, India, Italy, Norway, and Sweden (10–8).

Coordinating the efforts of this complex group was no easy task. Clearly, the problem would have been simplified if everyone had been like the British Commonwealth Brigade. The British, true professionals, were well trained and well equipped, and they soon set up their own supply lines and oriented their own units. Also, because the Commonwealth soldiers all spoke English, no linguistic or major communications problems arose. The forces of other nations, however, arrived in various stages of combat readiness, and many of their troops did not speak English.

Eventually, the establishment of a UN reception center alleviated the problem. At the center, experienced officers and NCOs provided useful combat orientation. At the same time, logisticians set up supply and maintenance procedures. Once the orientation had been accomplished and the units were judged ready for battle, they were normally attached to American outfits—the battalions to U.S. regiments and the brigades to U.S. divisions. The British Commonwealth forces were combined into brigades and attached to the U.S. I Corps. In general, the parent units provided administrative, logistical, and operational support and guidance. Amazingly, the system worked. On the whole, it was a matter of willing cooperation and plain common sense.

10–8 Staff officers of the 60th Indian Field Ambulance Unit at Taegu.

10–9 Lt. Col. John Hopkins, Commander, 1st Battalion, 5th Marine Regiment, leads a memorial service in the field.

Between June 1950 and July 1953, some 5.7 million Americans were in uniform, with about 1.5 million rotating in and out of Korea. American peak strength on the peninsula, however, never exceeded 348,000. Tragically, more than 54,000 Americans died in Korea, with 33,629 killed in action and 20,617 lost to other causes, such as plane crashes, disease, and vehicle accidents. In addition, 103,284 were wounded; this figure does not include the thousands of GIs who were slightly wounded, treated by medics, and returned to their units without their wounds being reported. It is worth noting that, although the number of American battle deaths in Korea was considerably less than the 47,000 battle deaths later in Vietnam, Korean losses took place during a three-year period and Vietnam losses occurred over a ten-year span (10–9).

Other UN casualties totaled about 3,000 killed and 12,000 wounded, with slightly more than half of these suffered by the Commonwealth forces (10–10). The ROK armed forces were hardest hit of all, with some 59,000 killed and 291,000 wounded. Korean civilian deaths, both North and South, probably exceeded 2 million. For the enemy, the best available data suggest that the Communists suffered between 1.25 million and 1.5 million killed, wounded, prisoners, or missing. By any account, the total number of civilian and military casualties is staggering.

Today, however, the unpredictable communist regime of North Korea still poses a threat. Consequently, since 1953, the United States has maintained a military presence in South Korea, a trip-wire force, which serves as a reminder that an unprovoked attack on South Korea will be regarded also as an attack on its American ally.

This American presence has not been without cost. Between 1966 and 1969, for example, perhaps emboldened by America's preoccupation with Vietnam, North Korea tested American resolve by waging what many historians consider the "Second Korean Conflict." During that period in Korea, U.S. casualties numbered 82 killed and 114 wounded. Also, 85 Americans were taken prisoner, 82 of them as a result of the illegal seizing in international waters of the USS *Pueblo*, an electronic "spy ship." After 1969, when it became clear to the communists that the United States was determined to remain in South Korea, the hostile activity diminished. From time to time, however, there have been other flare-ups, as in August 1976 when two American officers, members of a work party trimming a tree that blocked the view of the Demilitarized Zone, were set upon and beaten to death by a mob of North Korean soldiers. It remains clear that, despite the 1953 armistice, true peace on the Korean peninsula has yet to be achieved.

On May 1, 1990, President George Bush spoke of the significance of the Korean War. "It was," he said, "a war in which we turned the tide against Communism for the first time. Our defense of freedom laid the foundation for the march of democracy we're seeing today around the world."

To the Korean War veteran, even more poignant are the words of twenty-four-year-old Lt. William R. Penington, a platoon leader in the 32d Infantry Regiment of the 7th Division. In 1951, shortly before he was killed while leading his platoon, Bill Penington wrote home: " . . . if anything should happen to me, realize, as I

10–10 Men of the 61st Middlesex Regiment pray at a funeral service for three of their comrades.

10–11 61st National Athletic Competition, Seoul, 1998.

10–12 Downtown Seoul with a view of City Hall, 1999.

10–13 Po-hang Steel Company.

10–14 Modern agriculture.

do, that neither mine nor the other daily sacrifices being made in Korea are for any but a very worthy and important cause."

If Bill Penington were to visit South Korea today, he would not recognize the place, but he would like what he saw. South Korea is an economic miracle, America's seventh largest trading partner, and its staunchest ally. It has become the world's eleventh strongest economy and the fifth largest producer of automobiles. For once, in its long history, thanks to the sacrifices of such

men as Penington, South Korea has been able to act solely in its own national interest. As a result, it has produced an astounding level of prosperity and has become a vital, thriving country with modern schools, highways, skyscrapers, busy streets, and stores crammed with bountiful consumer goods (10–11 to 10–17). Its neighbor, North Korea, by contrast, remains an ugly, impoverished dictatorship, a saber-rattling outcast in the world of nations, and a continuing threat to world peace.

When the armistice was signed in 1953, China saw the war as a minor triumph, a standing up to America, and a reaffirmation of China's dominant role in East Asia. Since then, however, China has revised that view. As reported in *Newsweek* (July 14, 1997), the official Chinese Communist Party magazine, *Hundred Year Tide*, in a three-part series, portrayed Soviet leader Joseph Stalin as the Korean War's ultimate mastermind, Kim Il Sung as a naive radical who boasted that he could conquer the South "in two weeks," and Mao

Tse-tung as the man who went along against the advice of his top generals. Drawn from both Soviet and Chinese archives, the essays suggest that the war was not a "glorious victory," as China first proclaimed, but a blunder that played into Stalin's hands and undermined China's real interest in East Asia.

Although most Americans were relieved when the 1953 armistice was signed, they had mixed feelings about the war itself, an uneasiness about ending a war that was neither won nor lost. For the first time in history, the United States did not grant its returning veterans a heroes' welcome. During the years that followed, the country tended not to think much about Korea but, in fact, to make it "the forgotten war."

South Korea has *never* forgotten that war, of course. Not only have the South Koreans erected monuments (10–18) but, in recent years, they have hosted a program in which America's Korean War veterans are brought back to the "Land of the Morning Calm" to be honored and to see modern Korea for themselves.

Fortunately, at the fiftieth anniversary of the war's beginning, there is a new appreciation in the United States of American sacrifices and accomplishments during the Korean War. Monuments, such as one in Nashville near the Tennessee state capitol (10–19) and another in Pittsburgh, Pennsylvania (10–20), have been erected in cities and

10–15 Traditional Korean dance performed by young women to celebrate the coming harvest, 1999.

10–16 Chong Ro, Seoul's "Main Street," 1999.

10–18 Task Force Smith Monument, Osan, Korea.

10–17 Skyline of Seoul with Namsan Mountain in the background.

10–19 Korean War Memorial, Nashville, Tennessee.

10–20 Korean War Memorial, Pittsburgh, Pennsylvania.

10–21 and 10–22 Korean War Veterans Memorial, Washington, D.C.

towns across America. On July 27, 1995, the forty-second anniversary of the armistice, a Korean War Veterans Memorial was dedicated in Washington, D.C. to honor all who served in what should never be a "forgotten war." Congress authorized this national monument in 1986. Two years later, Ash Woods, located near the Lincoln Memorial, was selected as the construction site, and President Bush led a groundbreaking ceremony in 1992. It is essentially a garden memorial that includes a black granite wall with murals by Louis Nelson of New York City, a reflecting pool, and statues by sculptor Frank C. Gaylord that depict an infantry rifle platoon on an approach march in combat formation (10–21 and 10–22). Millions of visitors have seen the monument, admired it, and remembered the men and women who served their country during the Korean War.

1950

June 25	North Korean People's Army invades South Korea.
June 26	U.S. Ambassador John J. Muccio orders nonessential embassy personnel and all U.S. dependents evacuated to Japan.
June 27	President Harry S Truman authorizes U.S. air and naval operations south of the 38th Parallel. UN Security Council passes resolution declaring the NKPA attack to be a breach of world peace and calls on member nations to assist Republic of Korea in repelling aggression.
June 28	Seoul falls to NKPA.
June 29	President Truman authorizes bombing of North Korea and sea blockade of Korean coast.
June 30	President Truman authorizes sending of U.S. ground troops to Korea.
July 1	Task Force Smith (1st Battalion, 21st Infantry) arrives in Pusan.
July 4	United States Army in Korea (USAFIK) headquarters activated to control U.S. Army troops in Korea. Maj. Gen. William F. Dean assumes command of USAFIK in addition to command of 24th Infantry Division.
July 5	Task Force Smith engages NKPA at Osan.
July 6–8	34th Infantry Regiment, 24th Division, engages NKPA at Pyongtaek and Chonan.
July 7	UN Security Council resolution establishes UN Command.
July 8	President Truman appoints Gen. Douglas MacArthur as commander-in-chief of UN Command (CINCUNC)
July 8–12	21st Infantry Regiment, 24th Division, delays the advancing NKPA at Chochiwon but suffers heavy losses.
July 10–18	25th Infantry Division moves to Korea from bases in Japan.
July 13	U.S. Eighth Army assumes command of all U.S. ground forces in Korea, with Lt. Gen. Walton H. Walker in command.
July 14	South Korean President Syngman Rhee assigns control of ROK Armed Forces to General MacArthur. Battle of the Kum River.
July 18	Lead elements of 1st Cavalry Division land at Pohang.
July 20	Taejon falls to NKPA. General Dean reported missing.
July 24	Fifth Air Force relocates headquarters from Japan to Korea.
July 25	29th Regimental Combat Team (RCT) from Okinawa committed to combat near Chinju.
July 29	General Walker tells Eighth Army Troops to "stand or die."
July 31	5th RCT arrives in Korea from Japan.
August 1	Lead elements of 2d Infantry Division arrive in Korea from Fort Lewis, Washington.
August 2	1st Provisional Marine Brigade arrives in Korea from Camp Pendleton, California.
August 4	Pusan Perimeter established.
August 8–18	First battle of the Naktong Bulge.
August 10–20	ROK units battle for Pohang on east coast.
August 15–20	Battle for "Bowling Alley" west of Taegu. ROK 1st Division and U.S. 23d and 27th Infantry Regiments badly maul the attacking NKPA.
August 25	Japan Logistical Command established.
August 26	5th RCT assigned to 24th Infantry Division as replacement for decimated 34th Infantry Regiment.
August 29	British 27th Brigade arrives from Hong Kong.
August 31–September 19	Second battle of the Naktong Bulge.
September 15	D-day for Inchon invasion by Joint Task Force 7.

September 16–22	Eighth Army breaks out of Pusan Perimeter.
September 17	Kimpo airbase seized by 5th Marine Regiment; 1st Marine Aircraft Wing F-4U Corsairs land and begin operations ashore.
September 19	Louis Johnson resigns as Secretary of Defense and is replaced by Gen. George C. Marshall.
September 21	X Corps, commanded by Army Maj. Gen. Edward M. Almond, assumes command of all forces ashore in Inchon-Seoul area.
September 24–25	187th Airborne RCT landed at Kimpo airfield after arriving from Japan by sea on September 20.
September 26	Eighth Army elements of 7th Cavalry Regiment link up with elements of 31st Infantry Regiment, X Corps, near Osan.
September 27	Seoul liberated. President Truman authorizes operations north of 38th Parallel.
September 29	Seoul officially returned to ROK President Syngman Rhee by General MacArthur.
September 30	ROK 3d Division crosses 38th Parallel.
October 2	Chinese Premier Chou En-lai tells Indian ambassador that the Chinese will intervene if UN troops cross 38th Parallel.
October 3	With arrival of 3d Battalion, Royal Australian Regiment, the British 27th Brigade is renamed 27th British Commonwealth Brigade.
October 4	Chinese Premier Mao Tse-tung makes final decision to intervene in Korean War.
October 7	UN General Assembly passes resolution authorizing action north of 38th Parallel to establish a unified and democratic Korea.
October 9	1st Cavalry Division in the lead as Eighth Army crosses 38th Parallel.
October 10	ROK Army captures port city of Wonsan on Korea's east coast.
October 15	Truman and MacArthur meet at Wake Island.
October 17	ROK Army captures Hamhung and its port city of Hungnam.
October 19	North Korean capital of Pyongyang captured by ROK 1st Infantry Division and 1st Cavalry Division.
October 20	187th Airborne RCT makes parachute assault on Sukchon and Sunchon north of Pyongyang.
October 25	Chinese Communist Forces (CCF) launches first-phase offensive, attacks ROK Army north of Unsan.
October 26–28	1st Marine Division lands at Wonsan.
October 30	X Corps orders 1st Marine Division to replace ROK units in Chosin Reservoir area.
November 1	Eighth Army "high watermark" as 21st Infantry Regiment arrives 18 miles from Manchurian border town of Sinuiju.
November 1–2	8th Cavalry Regiment attacked by CCF near Unsan. After battle, CCF disappears into the hills.
November 2–7	7th Marine Regiment engages CCF south of Chosin Reservoir; after stiff fighting, CCF disappears.
November 5–17	3d Infantry Division lands at Wonsan.
November 6	CCF attacks Eighth Army forces north of Chongchon River.
November 8	Seventy-nine B-29 Superfortresses strike Yalu River bridges at Sinuiju. First aerial battle between jet aircraft, during which USAF Lt. Russell Brown, flying an F-80, shoots down a North Korean MiG-15.
November 21	17th Infantry Regiment, 7th Division, reaches Yalu River.
November 24	Eighth Army begins "home by Christmas" offensive.
November 25	CCF launches second-phase offensive on Eighth Army front and inflicts heavy casualties north of Chongchon River. Eighth Army begins withdrawal. CCF attacks 1st Marine Division on west side of Chosin Reservoir and 7th Infantry Division on east side.
December 5	UN forces evacuate Pyongyang.
December 9	Marines complete fighting breakout begun on November 27; along with 7th Division, withdraw into perimeter at Hungnam.

December 10–24	Evacuation from Hungnam by X Corps.
December 15	UN forces retreat below 38th Parallel.
December 23	Eighth Army Commander Lt. Gen. Walton H. Walker killed in jeep accident. Lt. Gen. Matthew B. Ridgway named to replace him.
December 31	CCF attacks along entire Eighth Army front in third-phase New Year's Eve offensive.

1951

January 3–4	Seoul evacuated by UN forces, which withdraw to general line of Pyongtaek-Wonju-Sanchok.
January 7	Eighth Army initiates strong reconnaissance probes to regain contact with CCF.
January 15	Operation Wolfhound reestablishes contact with CCF near Osan.
January 25	Operation Thunderbolt begins as UN and ROK forces advance north toward Han River.
January 31–February 17	2d Infantry Division, with attached French Battalion, heavily engaged at Chipyong-ni.
February 5	Operation Roundup—X Corps advance on eastern flank.
February 11–17	CCF fourth-phase offensive.
February 21	Operation Killer—general advance by U.S. IX and X Corps.
February 28	Last enemy resistance south of Han River collapses.
March 7	Operation Ripper—advance across the Han River by IX and X Corps.
March 14–15	Seoul retaken by Eighth Army.
April 5	Operation Rugged—general advance to Kansas Line begins.
April 11	General MacArthur relieved as supreme commander; Ridgway named to replace him.
April 14	Lt. Gen. James A. Van Fleet appointed Eighth Army commander to replace Ridgway.
April 22	CCF launches fifth-phase offensive. UN forces, after withdrawing to new defense line, halt CCF offensive north of Han River.
May 16–23	CCF launches second and final effort of fifth-phase offensive. UN forces halt the offensive, they resume their advance.
June 1	Operation Piledriver begins with advance toward Wyoming Line.
June 23	Soviet Union's Jacob Malik proposes cease-fire.
June 30	General Ridgway, on orders from Washington, broadcasts readiness to discuss an armistice.
July 10	Negotiations between UN forces and communists open at Kaesong.
August 22	Communists ask for apology for alleged "bombing raid." Talks suspended when request denied.
August 31	1st Marine Division opens assault in Punchbowl.
September 2	2d Infantry Division opens attack against Heartbreak and Bloody Ridges.
October 12	IX Corps advances to Jamestown Line.
October 15	2d Infantry Division takes Heartbreak Ridge.
October 25	Truce talks resume.
November 12	Ridgway orders Van Fleet to cease offensive operations and to begin active defense, Operation Ratkiller.

1952

January 1	Month-long artillery and air campaign begins against enemy positions.
January–April	Disorder in UN prison camps as screening of prisoners begins.
May 7	Prisoners at Koje-do camp seize Brig. Gen. Frances Dodd and hold him hostage until May 11.
May 12	Ridgway leaves Korea to take over NATO command from General Eisenhower. Lt. Gen. Mark W. Clark assumes command.
June 6	Beginning of Operation Counter to occupy eleven patrol bases.
June 14	All objectives of Operation Counter occupied by 45th Division.
December	Breakout attempt by prisoners at Pongam-do suppressed.

1953

February	Van Fleet returns to United States for retirement. Lt. Gen. Maxwell D. Taylor assumes command of Eighth Army.
April 20–26	Operation Little Switch exchanges sick and wounded POWs.
April 26	Armistice talks resume at Panmunjom.
May 28	CCF, in regimental strength, attacks five outposts in 25th Division sector.
June 10	CCF opens assault against ROK II Corps near Kumsong.
June 15–30	CCF attacks in I Corps sector and takes two outpost positions.
July 6–10	Fierce struggle for Pork Chop Hill.
July 13	Final CCF offensive begins.
July 19	Negotiations at Panmunjom reach agreement on all points.
July 20	New main line of resistance established by U.S. IX Corps and ROK II Corps along south bank of Kumsong River.
July 27	Armistice signed, ending three years of conflict.
August 5–September 6	Final exchange of POWs, Operation Big Switch.

SELECTED BIBLIOGRAPHY

Alexander Bevin. *Korea: The First War We Lost.* New York: Hippocrene, 1986.

Appleman, Roy E. *U.S. Army in the Korean War: South to the Naktong, North to the Yalu.* Washington, D.C.: Government Printing Office, 1961.

————. *East of Chosin: Entrapment and Breakout in Korea 1950.* College Station: Texas A&M University Press, 1987.

————. *Disaster in Korea: The Chinese Confront MacArthur.* College Station: Texas A&M University Press, 1987.

————. *Escaping the Trap: The U.S. Army X Corps in Northeast Korea, 1950.* College Station: Texas A&M University Press, 1990.

————. *Ridgway Duels for Korea.* College Station: Texas A&M University Press, 1990.

Blair, Clay. *The Forgotten War: America in Korea, 1950–1953.* New York: Times Books, 1987.

Brady, Jim. *The Coldest War.* New York: Orion Books, 1990.

Ent, Uzal W. *Fighting on the Brink: Defense of the Pusan Perimeter.* Paducah, Ky: Turner Publishing, 1996.

Fehrenbach, T. R. *This Kind of War: A Study in Unpreparedness.* New York: Macmillan, 1963.

Flint, Roy K. "Task Force Smith and the 24th Division," in *America's First Battles 1776–1965,* edited by Charles E. Heller and William A. Stofft. Lawrence: University Press of Kansas, 1986.

Futrell, Robert F. *The United States Air Force in Korea: 1950–1953,* rev. ed. Washington, D.C.: Government Printing Office, 1983.

Goulden, Joseph. *Korea: The Untold Story of the War.* New York: Times Books, 1982.

Gugeler, Russell A., ed. *Combat Actions in Korea.* Washington, D.C.: Combat Forces Press, 1954.

Halliday, Jon, and Bruce Cumings. *Korea, the Unknown War.* New York: Pantheon Books, 1988.

Hallion, Richard P. *The Naval Air War in Korea.* Baltimore: The Nautical & Aviation Publishing Co. of America, 1986.

Hastings, Max. *The Korean War.* New York: Simon & Schuster, 1987.

Hermes, Walter G. *U.S. Army in the Korean War: Truce Tent and Fighting Front.* Washington, D.C.: Government Printing Office, 1966.

Hoyt, Edwin P. *The Pusan Perimeter.* New York: Stein & Day, 1984.

————. *The Bloody Road to Panmunjom.* New York: Stein & Day, 1985.

Knox, Donald. *The Korean War: An Oral History; from Pusan to Chosin.* New York: Harcourt Brace Jovanovich, 1985.

MacDonald, Callum A. *Korea: The War before Vietnam.* New York: Macmillan, 1986.

Maihafer, Harry J. *From the Hudson to the Yalu: West Point '49 in the Korean War.* College Station: Texas A&M University Press, 1993.

Marshall, S. L. A. *Pork Chop Hill—The American Fighting Man in Action—Korea, Spring 1953.* New York: William Morrow & Co., 1956.

———. *The River and the Gauntlet.* Westport, Conn.: Greenwood Press, 1970.

———. *The Military History of the Korean War.* New York: Franklin Watts, Inc., 1963.

McCullough, David. *Truman.* New York: Simon & Schuster, 1992.

Mossman, Billy C. *Ebb and Flow: The U.S. Army in the Korean War.* Washington, D.C.: Center of Military History, 1990.

Owen, Joseph R. *Colder than Hell: A Marine Rifle Company at Chosin Reservoir.* Annapolis, Md.: Naval Institute Press, 1996.

Paik, Sun Yup. *From Pusan to Panmunjom.* Washington: Brassey's, 1992.

Register of Graduates and Former Cadets of the United States Military Academy. West Point, NY: USMA Association of Graduates, 1998.

Ridgway, Matthew B. *The Korean War.* Garden City, N.Y.: Doubleday, 1967.

Sheldon, Walter J. *Hell or High Water: MacArthur's Landing at Inchon.* New York: Macmillan, 1968.

Spanier, John W. *The Truman-MacArthur Controversy and the Korean War.* New York: W. W. Norton, 1965.

Stokesbury, James L. *A Short History of the Korean War.* New York: William Morrow & Co., 1998.

Summers, Harry G. *Korean War Almanac.* New York: Facts on File, 1990.

Toland, John. *In Mortal Combat: Korea 1950–1953.* New York: William Morrow & Co., 1991.

United States Marine Corps. *U.S. Marine Operations in Korea, 1950–1953.* Washington, D.C.: U.S. Marine Corps, 1954.

Westover, John G. *Combat Support in Korea: The United States Army in the Korean Conflict.* Washington, D.C.: Center of Military History, 1955.

Whelan, Richard. *Drawing the Line: The Korean War.* Boston: Little, Brown, 1990.

f indicates figures (photographs)

ABOUT THE AUTHORS

Donald M. Goldstein, Ph.D. (University of Denver), is a professor of public and international affairs at the University of Pittsburgh and a former U.S. Air Force officer.

Harry J. Maihafer, a retired U.S. Army colonel and former banker, who lives in Nashville, Tennessee, holds a master's degree in journalism from the University of Missouri. During the Korean War, he served as an infantry platoon leader and as an aide to the commanding general of the 24th Infantry Division.